D0283419

5

REALLY BAD NEWS

REALLY BAD NEWS

Greg Philo   John Hewitt
Peter Beharrell   Howard Davis

(members of the
Glasgow University Media Group)

Writers and Readers

London   New York   Toronto   Sydney

Writers and Readers Publishing Cooperative Society Ltd.
144 Camden High Street, London NW1 0NE
England
Suite 814, 175 Fifth Avenue, New York, N.Y. 10010
U.S.A.

Published by Writers and Readers Publishing Cooperative Society
Ltd., 1982

Copyright © 1982 Greg Philo, John Hewitt, Peter Beharrell,
Howard Davis

Printed in Great Britain by
Redwood Burn Ltd, Trowbridge, Wiltshire
and bound by Pegasus Bookbinding, Melksham, Wiltshire.

Set in 11/12 Garamond by Shanta Thawani 01-889 0079 and
Anthony Richard Associates 01-361 1811

All rights reserved

This book is sold subject to the condition that it shall not, by way
of trade or otherwise, be lent, re-sold, hired out, or otherwise
circulated without the publisher's prior consent in any form of
binding or cover other than that in which it is published and
without a similar condition including this condition being
imposed on the subsequent purchaser.

".. SURPRISING NEWS FROM RHODESIA, WHERE ROBERT MUGABE, A MARXIST GUERRILLA, HAS DEFEATED ..."

"... AND SURPRISING NEWS FROM FRANCE, WHERE FRANÇOIS MITTERRAND, A SOCIALIST, HAS JUST BEEN ELECTED ..."

".. AND SURPRISING RIOTS IN LIVERPOOL, LONDON, MANCHESTER AND BRISTOL ..."

"... AND IN NORTHERN IRELAND, A SURPRISE RESULT IN FERMANAGH, WHERE BOBBY SANDS ...."

".. AND THAT'S ALL THE SURPRISING NEWS FROM US TONIGHT. GOODNIGHT."

CONTENTS

ACKNOWLEDGEMENTS

We would like to thank all those who have at different times worked with the group — original members Jean Hart, Alison McNaughton, Paul Walton and Brian Winston. We would also like to thank especially John Eldridge who has been a great source of help and encouragement, and has done much to contribute to this volume. Thanks also to students at Glasgow University who have helped in the work, especially James Duffy for his help on the Labour Party Study, and Jenny Buchanan, Lilian Weir, Graham Taylor and Kate Phillips. We thank also the people who have helped in the production of this book, Paul Taylor and Parlan McFarlane for photographs, also Ray Lowry, Colin Wheeler, Brian McAlister and John Minnion for cartoons. Thanks especially to Dominic D'Angelo for producing these and other drawings for us at a pace and level of expertise which was unsurpassed. Thanks also to Kathleen Davidson for her endless patience and deciphering abilities in preparing and typing the manuscript and also to Lily Lynes for making sparkling contributions.

There are many who have helped us with advice and information. Thanks especially to Dave Jordan of the Low Pay Unit; Toni Griffiths of NALGO and NUT; Jimmy Milne of the Scottish TUC; Alan Sapper at ACTT; Barry Almond and Norman West of Barnsley Labour Party; Anna Coote and Bruce Page of the *New Statesman*; Brian McArthur of *The Times*; Carl Gardner and John Wyver of *City Limits*; James Curran and Geoff Sheridan of the Campaign for Press Freedom; Alan Horrocks, Alex Graham and Greg Lanning of the Changing Television Group; Lisa Appignanesi and Karel

Clapshaw of Writers and Readers. Thanks also to Austin Mitchell, Phillip Whitehead, Michael Meacher, John Maxton, Tony Benn, Eric Heffer, Michael Foot, Janey Buchan, Norman Buchan, Chris Mullin, Jon Lansman and Brian Sedgemore.

Thanks also to our many academic colleagues and friends who have helped with discussion and criticism in the Sociology Departments of the University of Glasgow, City of Liverpool College of Higher Education and the University of Kent; to Gillian Skirrow, Stuart Hall, Alan Clarke, John Clarke, Jock Young, Mike Gonzales and especially to Lewis Minken and David Howell for advice on Labour Party coverage, and to Colonel J. Ditton, the equipment officer at Glasgow, for keeping us in milk, stamps and video recorders.

There are also many people who have been close to us and have helped by listening, contributing ideas and putting up with us. Special thanks here to Valerie Thomson, Joyce Wilson, Rene and Dick Philo and Des McNulty for not complaining (at least not very much), and to Stella McGarrity for timely help and Barbara Miller for help through some purple patches.

Finally we have many friends, associates and advisers who work inside television and have helped enormously. Thanks very much to them — we will leave them nameless, lest it end up in their personal file.

PREFACE

In this book we have built on the arguments and conclusions of the Glasgow University Media Group over the last six years. The group was originally set up with a grant from the Social Science Research Council to undertake a study of television news. We recorded news programmes over a six month period, focusing mainly on coverage of industry and the economy. This was one of the largest continuous samples of news output ever analysed and we spent much of the following three years on this task. Our conclusion was that television is biased to the extent that it violates its formal obligations to give a balanced account.

Our research also led us to discover that the broadcasting institutions are extremely hierarchical, that close links exist between them and a range of 'official' and 'acceptable' sources. The result of this is that the news gives a preferential treatment to some ways of seeing the world.

Over the last few years we have engaged in further studies which provide more proof for our initial conclusion. We have included this new material here, together with the conclusions of our 1975 work.

Our most recent work has been to investigate how politics is represented on television and analyse the relationship between news and current affairs programmes, as well as how the press relates to television. Our studies have led us to reflect on the historical and social factors which shape television's view of the world. We have given an account of this here, together with suggestions on how we might move towards a system of democratic broadcasting.

I
"AND NOW . . . THE NEWS"

Television is the most important source of news in our society.
It has now far outstripped the press as the main source of
information. Each night the two main bulletins on BBC 1 and
ITN alone have an estimated 16 million viewers. Television is
often judged to be accurate and reliable as compared with other
media. Television producers claim that they are impartial. We
have argued that they are not. But if they are not, does it really
make any difference?

It is sometimes argued that people simply make up their own
minds and are not influenced very much by what they read or
see. Our own view is that television cannot exclusively shape
people's thoughts or actions. Nonetheless it has a profound
effect, because it has the power to tell people the *order* in which
to think about events and issues. In other words it 'sets the
agenda', decides what is important and what will be featured.
More crucially it very largely decides what people will think
with: television controls the crucial information with which we
make up our minds about the world.

For example, people who work in car plants might know
that there are many reasons why their industry is in decline and
why production is lost. But those who take their information
from television are likely to focus on a narrower range of
causes. There are many people who have never worked in a
factory, who are sure that the main problem is strikes. When
we analysed the coverage of British Leyland we found that the
news persistently presented these as the main cause of lost
production and stoppages. Yet in that period, half of the total
stoppages were caused by factors *other* than strikes at Leyland,

such as machine breakdown or mistakes by management. Yet
on television, we found that the word 'stoppage' and the word
'strike' were interchangeable. "Another stoppage at Leyland",
was likely to be automatically interpreted by viewers as a
reference to a strike.

"...AND TONIGHT ON 'NATIONWIDE', AS
IRAN DECLARES WAR ON CHINA, AND
UNEMPLOYMENT REACHES FOUR MILLION,
WE ASK, WHAT ABOUT THAT ROYAL
BABY?"

In the same way we found that wage increases were treated as
the main cause of inflation. In fact the two words became
almost synonymous on the news. Yet there were many other
causes of inflation in this period. People were forced to pay
higher prices for land, houses and rents as a result of the
speculative boom in property in the early seventies. Yet
property speculators were not consistently pilloried on the
news nor their actions positively held up as the cause of rising
prices. Trade unionists were: month after month the figures
for wage increases were compared with price rises as if the one
automatically caused the other. The *information* that there are
causes of inflation other than wage increases was often not
provided. It was thus made easy for viewers to reach the
conclusion that wages and unions were to blame for inflation.
When we showed our results at trade union schools and
conferences we found that people believed that wages had shot
up and had caused inflation. This was so even when they
believed their *own* wages had fallen in real terms. This apparent
contradiction was resolved time and time again by each
individual group of trade unionists saying that while *their*
wages had fallen *other* people's must have gone up. They
tended to believe the news account of reality even where it

differed from their own immediate experience. While the wages of a few groups, such as the miners, had indeed risen and were the focus of a great deal of news coverage, the mass of working people had actually taken a cut in their real wages.

While strikes and wage increases are routinely referred to on the news as the cause of economic problems, there is no systematic examination of other areas of the economy which may cause difficulties. For instance, references to private investment as a problem area, if they occur at all, appear only as fragments. Unless we are informed what under-investment means, what it causes, and what has happened to the money that might have been invested in industry, then it is difficult to 'make up our minds' about what is really wrong. When the Conservative government removed exchange controls in 1979, over the next two years 4,500 million pounds was swept out of this country to be invested abroad. Much of this has gone into property, or has gone to countries such as South Africa where very high returns can be made from cheap, controlled labour. But this information is hardly prominent in the news. Where are all the headlines which could have read:

WE WAS ROBBED — Three Million Unemployed as Capital Flows Abroad.

There is no routine reporting by the news of this form of damage to the economy. The lack of investment means that machinery and plant becomes more obsolete and industry becomes more uncompetitive. But there are no outraged consumers on the news, asked about the movements of high finance. There is no analysis of this sort of problem which is comparable to the way that strikes are endlessly and routinely reported.

To the extent that news controls such explanations, it is ideological: a way of seeing and understanding the world which favours some interests over others.

The Glasgow Work*

In the first stages of our analysis we compared the picture of the industrial world which television news creates with those of other sources, including official statistics on employment, strikes and accident rates. Later we made detailed studies of the language used in industrial reporting, and we examined the routine ways of presenting film and other visual material. Finally, we selected several stories and issues which recéived a large and sustained amount of coverage and showed how the whole range of factors involved in news manufacture leads quite consistently to a highly partial and distorted view of relations within industry and within society generally.

Our initial work showed that all three television channels offer a remarkably similar product. The number of stories they run from day to day, the types of stories and the presentation of the stories (the running order, who appears, use of film, *etc.*) only vary within very narrow limits. The people who make television news share the same ideas and routines of production in whichever organisation they work. This leads to great predictability and sameness in the product. Essentially, it is the minor differences of style rather than the news content which give people the impression that the BBC and ITN offer different kinds of news.

---

* Our findings were originally presented as a report to the Social Science Research Council and detailed versions of them have since appeared in *Bad News* (Routledge and Kegan Paul, 1976) and *More Bad News* (Routledge and Kegan Paul, 1980).

Our analysis of industrial news provided overwhelming evidence for the selectivity of news about industrial life and our study of it shows how certain industries and activities are emphasised to the near total neglect of others. In the first six months of 1975, half of all the industrial stories in the bulletin concerned just three categories of industry — transport and communication, public administration and, overwhelmingly, the motor manufacturing industry. The relatively small fraction of Britain's workforce who make vehicles (just over 2 per cent) had nearly *one quarter* of the general industrial coverage on television news. The coverage of strikes reveals a concentration amounting to distortion. For example, the engineering industry, which had a high incidence of strikes in the period of our study, received negligible coverage. Of the 20 principal disputes (those singled out by the Department of Employment as being particularly significant for the economy), 9 were never mentioned at all on the television news. It could be argued that such concentration is excusable if it allows more time for close and careful reporting of the selected stories, but our subsequent research shows that *more* does not usually mean *better* in running stories which attract extended coverage.

In our study of the language of industrial news reporting over a four month period there is further evidence of a failure to maintain balance and impartiality. This is partly because of what is said and partly because of what is left unsaid. For instance, the causes of strikes and disputes are not reported consistently. Consequently, the details which *are* regularly given — time, place and numbers involved — do not fit into a coherent sequence of events and extended negotiation. Instead the impression is created of random, meaningless acts which break out in an otherwise peaceful and ordered society. Even the simple descriptive terms like 'dispute' are consistently used in a way which implies that labour is the source of the conflict within industry. So one hears of the 'dustcart drivers' dispute', the 'civil servants' dispute' or the 'laggers' dispute' without reference to the other 'side' who are the employers and the government. Some might say that these groups could be responsible for disputes by, for example, seeking to impose lower wages, redundancies or longer hours. But on the news, 'trouble' is more likely to come from low status or marginal groups — from the bottom of society rather than the 'top'. In this example from BBC news a variety of quite different groups and situations are simply lumped together in the general theme of trouble, rumblings and unrest from the working class.

> The week had its share of unrest. Trouble in Glasgow with striking dustmen and ambulance controllers, short time in the car industry, no *Sunday Mirror* or *Sunday People* today and *a fair amount of general trouble* in Fleet Street and a *continuing rumbling* over the matter of two builders' pickets jailed for conspiracy.
>
> (BBC 2 18:55 19.1.75 Our italics*)

: .. Tonight's "Any Questions" comes as usual from the Thornliebank and District Conservative Association, Knutsford, with a discussion on "Rumblings from the Working Class" "...

It is sometimes said by broadcasters and others that television news is compelled to choose dramatic and visually exciting news wherever possible, because television is a 'visual' medium. Sometimes they even imply that this 'visual imperative' is an excuse for departures from the norm of balance and impartiality. Our study of the visual content of the news — (an analysis of every single change of shot in one week's news in May 1975) — leads to two main conclusions which have consequences for news bias. Firstly, the visual aspects of news presentation do not determine whether or not stories are run or how much attention or importance they are given. Many of

---

*Italics in quotations throughout this book denote our own emphases.

the most important stories are not very 'visual' anyway and consist largely of 'talking heads' (shots of people talking directly to camera or being interviewed). This is especially true of political, industrial and economic coverage and inadequacies in these areas are not caused by the search for visually exciting material. Secondly, what happens in practice is that the news will look for the most visually interesting shots within the limits that govern the particular story and what will normally be said about it. The real question is what determines these limits? Why for example are the cameras outside the factory filming pickets, with a commentary by a journalist on 'law and order', rather than inside the factory filming graphic evidence of management mistakes?

Our work overall suggested that the television news represents a coherent and partisan position. We found, for example, that:

— In the 13 weeks of the Glasgow dustcart drivers' strike, which was reported in 102 bulletins and included 20 interviews, not once did a striker get to state his case nationally in an interview.

— In the same story from Glasgow, the causes of the strike were mentioned only 11 times out of 40 items on BBC 1, 6 times out of 19 on BBC 2 and 19 times out of 43 mentions on ITN.

In January 1975 a widely reported speech by the Prime Minister which referred to "manifestly avoidable stoppages of production" caused by management and labour was transformed in 29 later references, and made to apply to the workforce alone. This was part of the general view given that 'the ills of British Leyland' could be laid substantially at the door of the labour force.

— In the coverage of the strike by engine tuners at Cowley, as against BBC 1's 22 references to Leyland's 'strike problem', there were only 5 references to 'management failings' and 1 to the Company's investment record. On BBC 2 there were 8 references to strikes as against 3 to management and 2 to investment; on ITN 33 to strikes, 8 to management, and none to investment.

— In the first four months of 1975 there were 17 occasions when views were presented on the news against the government's policy of wage restraint and lower wages as a solution to the economic crisis. There were 287 occasions when views supporting these policies were broadcast.

News Sense

The news is a manufactured product that is organised and constructed from within very limited ways of seeing the world. One TV news reporter described to us how during the period of the 'Winter of Discontent' in 1979 he had spent a week looking for dead chickens. At the time stories were circulating that animals were dying through lack of feed, following the strike of the lorry drivers. We asked him if the search had been successful, and he described how he had combed every chicken farm from coast to coast looking for one that was even sickly. But did he find any? He replied that there had been 25 dead chickens. A camera team had been installed in a chicken coop to get shots for the story — the equipment was ready and cables installed. Finally they were ready to roll and switched on all the lights. Twenty-five chickens died of shock. To his knowledge these were the only chickens to have died in the lorry drivers' dispute. While this reporter was searching for dead chickens others were looking for empty supermarket shelves as the effects of the dispute were exaggerated in the media.

In such selection and organisation, the news follows a narrow set of ideas and interests, and these determine what descriptions are made of events. These may vary depending on whose interests are at stake. We all know that strikes are bad, unless they happen in Poland. The news neglects to tell us that if British workers acted in the same way as their Polish counterparts, they would be breaking the provisions of the Conservative government's Employment Act. Poland in Britain would very definitely be reported as:

MORE VIOLENCE OUTSIDE FACTORIES AS FLYING PICKETS FIGHT POLICE.

Television news tends to speak in terms of 'one community' and 'one nation'. But it is clear that different rules apply for describing different sections of our society. These depend on whether you are powerful or weak, a man or a woman, and black or white. In 1980 thirteen children died in a terrible fire during a party in Deptford. It is not hard to imagine what the coverage of this event would have been like had the children been white. The tragedy of each victim would have been outlined — their parents, their hopes, their prospects — young lives cut short. But the victims were black and overtones were of racial violence, and one reporter asked white residents if it had been a 'noisy party'. More usually, the black community tends to be under-represented unless there is a 'problem'. Then, they are likely to be presented as creating difficulties for white people, not as themselves having problems through living in a racist society. They are spoken of in the context of debates about 'immigration', 'repatriation' and Britain as having a 'race problem'.

News sense also has a male bias. Our study of 1975 showed that only 8% of all named interviewees were women. The mass of these are involved in sport, disasters, or are Margaret Thatcher or the Queen.

Who Makes it That Way?

The downgrading of women and black people in television coverage is reflected by their under-representation. In Thames Television in 1981 there were 55 producers, directors, researchers and reporters working in current affairs and documentaries (excluding Thames News). There are no black people in this group which comprises 37 men and 18 women. But of the men, 22 are producers and directors, while only three women are in this category. In addition, on Thames News — a service which covers Brixton, Southall and Lewisham — there are over 50 programme staff, but only one black person is employed. A different survey of three ITV companies revealed that of the 74 producer/directors of *Weekend World*, *TV Eye* and *World in Action*, only ten were women. A similar situation prevails on the technical side of broadcasting. In 1978 of the 360 people recruited by the BBC for technical posts, only 10 women were appointed.

The broadcasting institutions, and especially the BBC, are thoroughly hierarchical. The higher up one goes, the more likely it is that people will be drawn from the established channels of power and influence. The composition of the Boards of Governors of the BBC and IBA illustrate a long tradition of appointing men (and occasionally women) from the good and worthy sectors of Britain's upper classes. In the BBC the Chairman is the owner of the Castle Howard stately home and ex-President of the Country Landowners

Association. Other governors include the former editor of *The Times*; an ex-Presbyterian Minister now Director of a University; a former High Commissioner for Canada; a university professor; the director of Littlewood's Pools; a chartered accountant; a former chairman of the Headteachers Association; and a former Minister of State. The member with special responsibility for Northern Ireland is the wife of a Protestant ex-Prime Minister of Northern Ireland. Where trade unionists are appointed they have tended to be less than radical in their affiliations. At present we have Lord Allen of Fallowfield. There is also one black woman, recently appointed, who was formerly the General Secretary of the Campaign against Racial Discrimination.

For the IBA Board, the Chairman is Lord Thomson of Monifieth. Other members include the Managing Director of Guinness; the Managing Director of Alcan Aluminium; a Director of Credit Suisse First Boston Ltd; the Chaplain to the Queen in Scotland; two university professors and a senior research fellow from Oxford University; a JP who is an ex-shopping editor of *House and Garden* and the Marchioness of Anglesey (ex-chairwoman of the National Federation of Women's Institutes). The member for Northern Ireland is a barrister and wife of a former Minister in the Stormont Parliament. From the unions there is the General Secretary of the Inland Revenue Staff Association.

The predominant character of these boards is white middle class and male with a high proportion from public schools and Oxford and Cambridge. They are not in any sense 'balanced', but are extremely establishment oriented. We are not suggesting that a right-wing oligarchy should be replaced by one that is left-wing. The issues are to make broadcasting representative of society, to give access to a range of groups at its base and to let people really speak for themselves. This will not be achieved by a broadcasting system controlled by governors and senior administrators who operate as a cultural elite. This elite sets limits on what their employees are allowed to do or say. Not everyone in these companies wishes to diverge from these limits, and given the background and training of most journalists, this is hardly surprising. But even where individuals *are* critical, it is very difficult to break from 'normal' journalism and the 'acceptable' house style, since

there are always pressures from the top to conform. No
journalist or producer can fight every battle which comes
along: in the end the most effective form of control is self-
censorship. In the BBC the production of 'correct' journalism
is constantly monitored in News and Current Affairs
meetings. These involve the top thirty producers together
with the Director General and various assistants. They may
comment on past lapses or current practice and may also offer
helpful hints on future programmes. For example when our
first criticisms of the BBC appeared, the Director General
suggested an attack be mounted on sociology as a whole:

> The Director General said there would be no sense in attacking
> Bad News in detail . . . he thought however that the ideology of
> sociologists was a subject which would repay a little study and
> hoped that it would be possible for a programme like 'Analysis'
> to tacke it.

(BBC Confidential News and Current Affairs Minutes 24.9.76)
Both the BBC and IBA have intervened directly on many
occasions to censor or halt programmes, particularly in
'sensitive' areas such as coverage of Northern Ireland.

The direct control of programmes from the top extends
beyond news and current affairs. There has been a series of
bitter rows about the banning of plays such as *The War Game*,
Scum, and *Solid Geometry*. The row over *The War Game* was
obviously political. However, many of these 'censorship'
arguments are conducted on an absolutely ludicrous level,
such as the number of swearwords per half an hour which the
BBC will allow. The priority of the administrators is to defend
the institution as such. The apparent arbitrariness of many
decisions comes from their desire to placate any group who
they see as a threat — from politicians through to the Viewers
and Listeners' Association. David Hare recently commented
about his own experiences in the drama department:

> Programme makers no longer feel that the bureacracy sees its
> job as to serve them. Instead they feel that they themselves have
> been made the servants of a corporation which is organised
> chiefly for the convenience of its own executive, and whose
> incidental product happens by chance to be television
> programmes.
>
> As a film-maker, when I receive any message from above, my
> immediate reaction is that I must be in trouble, for I can imagine

no other reason why they are trying to contact me. If I hear one
of the great panjandra wants to talk to me, I assume
automatically that his purpose will be to unveil a fresh scheme
for butchering my work. ... They believe that by placating
politicians, they will ensure the survival of public broadcasting.

(The Guardian 15.8.81)

A further pressure on journalists to stay in line — and this
separates them from most people — is simply that they are
very well treated financially. On average a reporter or producer
at the BBC will earn around £15,000, while a producer at an
Independent company will receive upwards of £26,000 per
year, plus expenses for hotels and restaurants, etc. Their style
of life is quite distinct from many of those on whom they
report. When the Warrington by-election of July 1981 was
announced, the joke which went around the BBC for the next
two days was 'how does one eat in that part of the world?' Such
differences are important since they create immense problems
for journalists as professionals. Most have few experiences
outside their own class and culture and are not well placed to
speak about what it is like to be unemployed or to be
scrutinised for cohabitation by social security investigators.
This cultural clash becomes apparent when programmes on
such areas are made. For example a BBC Panorama entitled
"The Real Unemployed" was genuinely intended as a sensitive
analysis of people who had been out of work for long periods.
One section involved an interview between a Glasgow man in a
run down council estate and a BBC reporter. The exchange
shows the chasm across which both are talking to each other:

REPORTER: (This person) is forty-eight. Long ago, he worked
on the buses. He's been out of a job for years. Work has now
been replaced with pigeons.

REPORTER: Is this your hobby — pigeon-breeding?

MAN: . . . I've nothing else to do . . . not a lot you know.

REPORTER: How many children do you have?

MAN: There's two divorced and with the ones you saw this
morning, thirteen.

REPORTER: Thirteen. How do you manage to exist, how do
you manage financially?

MAN: Well, we just get by, you know, with Family Allowance.

REPORTER: How much do you get altogether?

MAN: Forty pounds (counts) twenty-eight pounds . . . so that's

sixty-eight pounds, uh?
REPORTER: You get sixty-eight pounds a week? *That's quite a
lot, isn't it?* Enough to live off?
                              (BBC 1 *Panorama* 19.5.80)
Sixty-eight pounds would represent approximately one day's
expenses for a reporter in an ITV company (a BBC reporter
would get less). It is unacceptable for middle class journalists
to suggest that it is a reasonable amount for thirteen people to
live on for a week. The Head of *Panorama* commented to us
that the question was included because it was of the sort that
'viewers wanted to hear about'. Whatever the intention of the
producers the effect of such a question is simply to drag up a
range of prejudices about people on social security which have
already been firmly established in the right-wing press.

Open Door for the Powerful

The backgrounds of most journalists in broadcasting and the
world in which they live mean that they share a common
culture with the most powerful groups and interests in our
society. Furthermore, official sources such as the Treasury and
the Ministry of Defence gain routine access for their views on
television, since they have the power to make sure that their
voices are heard. In a sense they control the livelihood of
journalists, since given the type of news journalists have to
produce, these sources have a monopoly over certain kinds of
information. For example, they might leak the content of
cabinet discussions. Press briefings are given to favoured
journalists and the more powerful the interests that are at
stake, the more tightly will the vision be controlled. The
Ministry of Defence for example has more press and
information personnel than any other Government department (including the Central Office of Information). Senior
news journalists in this area tend to have a very close affinity
with these interests and sometimes have a military background
themselves. In order to see the world from such standpoints,
the news sometimes requires us to turn somersaults with our
values and exclude or downgrade alternative views.
    For example, there is at present a rising current of opinion
which does not see European and American defence interests
as being synonymous. The new Campaigns for Nuclear

Disarmament in Britain and Europe have come, not from any liking or trust of the Soviet Union, but from an increasing distrust of American foreign policy. This has arisen in the wake of the Vietnam War, El Salvador and the increasingly 'hawkish' stance of American military leaders. In addition, nuclear war has become more of a possibility with the development of bombs whose effects can be confined to very limited areas or 'theatres'. The new fear is that the chosen 'theatre' will be Europe, with its proliferation of American bases right up to the borders of the Soviet Union. These fears were given some real grounds by an ex-Pentagon strategic planner, Rear Admiral Jean le Roque, who commented:

> We fought World War One in Europe, we fought World War Two in Europe, and if you dummies will let us we will fight World War Three in Europe as well.   (*Guardian*, 26.2.81)

Where television criticisms have been made of American policy they tend to occur in one-off current affairs programmes (e.g. *Panorama* 18.5.81). Television news does not routinely acknowledge such views or begin from the assumption that 103 American bases in Britain *may* or *may not* be a good thing. The vision of the world in 'defence news' is largely constricted to what is good or bad for NATO. We all know that democracy is a good thing, especially if it occurs in Poland and therefore upsets the Soviet Union. But for the BBC the collapse of democracy in Turkey following a military coup is not such a bad thing after all, especially since it will 'aggrieve Moscow' and should therefore occasion only 'a few crocodile tears'.

> Turkey has an enormous army, much bigger than Britain's for instance, but it's the geographical position of the country that matters so much. Turkey has a long border with the Soviet Union on the Southern flank of NATO. And the West have been watching with gloom the troubles building up there. So *putting aside a few crocodile tears about democracy*, most Western observers are quietly pleased that the military is now in charge in Ankara. And the whole region looks that much more stable tonight than it did last night. Particularly since it may improve the prospects of Greece returning fully to the NATO fold. The Russians, inevitably perhaps, suspect the Americans of a hand in this coup. Apart from the former Turkish Government, Moscow is probably the most aggrieved by it all.
> (BBC 1 21.00 12.9.80)

At this time Turkey had deeply rooted social problems: a high level of unemployment, imminent economic collapse and political violence. But it is not at all clear that a takeover by the Army was the best solution for the problems of the mass of the people. There were a number of points of view on this. The *New Statesman* carried an article on 19.9.80 entitled "Turkish Generals are the Disease not the Cure".

Civil war and political violence are indeed disastrous. However, from the point of view advanced by ITN, the problem is not the effect of these on the people involved, but again it is the difficulties that are raised for NATO. The advantage of the generals is that they will once again 'get the place under control' and Turkey's front line role against the Russians will be secure:

> In a country as strategically placed as Turkey civil war would have been disastrous. She's the only member of NATO, apart from Norway, who shares a common border with the Soviet Union, as well as controlling the only way in and out of the Black Sea, so vital to the Russians. Turkey is also at the end of the so-called Crescent of Crisis, which includes Iran and Afghanistan — so it's not somewhere that NATO wants to see weakened by civil war.

(ITN 22:00 12.9.80)

" . . . and now, Defence news, supplied by the North Atlantic Treaty Organisation . . . "

This approach to 'defence' interests even extends to coverage of South Africa where the press and broadcasting in general has a fairly liberal record. On the same night as the coverage of Turkey the BBC showed what was effectively a propaganda film for the re-opening of the Simonstown base in South Africa which had previously been closed by a Labour government. The tenuous excuse for this piece of 'news' is that the South Africans are 'hinting' about it. With the help of the BBC they are able to drop very heavy hints indeed:

> While NATO forces work on their European defence plans, worries about the Cape oil route still exercise the minds of some Western leaders. Until five years ago, the South African naval base of Simonstown played a vital part in Britain's defence thinking. The Labour Government ended that link — *but now the South Africans are hinting* that the West might like to think again about Simonstown.

(BBC 1 21:00 12.9.80)

There follows a description of the history of the base and South Africa's preparation to repel black African navies. The report then becomes simply a commercial about what a "marvellous base" it has been and the following conversation is shown over shots of happy South African sailors jumping into swimming pools:

> BBC REPORTER: Simonstown has been in the past, and traditionally, *a marvellous base* for other navies as well, but has it still got that potential to offer facilities for navies working in the Indian Ocean area?
> SOUTH AFRICAN NAVAL OFFICER: Well I think, at the moment it's a fantastic base for our Navy. We have, as you saw today, recently enlarged . . . the harbour to quite some considerable extent, it's got more than twice the berthing facilities as it had before. We're also building new workshops and repair facilities — we can look after ourselves very well.
> BBC REPORTER: It's these resources, plus the recreational opportunities for sailors after periods at sea, that South Africa appears to be offering.

(BBC 1 21:00 12.9.80)

Television news gives a partial view of the world: it offers an open door to the powerful and a closed door to the rest of us. In this way it violates its own proclaimed principles of fairness and objectivity. In the chapters which follow we show how many of its favoured themes directly parallel those in the private and openly partisan press. It is distinguished from this mainly by its politer style and the inclusion of token nods in the direction of alternative thought. This is a long way from being a 'public service'.

II
"AND NOW THEY'RE OUT AGAIN"
Industrial Coverage

Most meetings are at 7.30 as we start work. Being on strike, the unions fixed them all for two hours later, which gave us time to read the papers and listen to the radio and in the end the morale went.
(BL worker on the defeat of the 1981 Leyland strike.
The Guardian, 4.11.81)

When we began our research we were interested in the picture given of the industrial world: of what were presented as its problems and potential solutions. Our method was to look first at the *possible* explanations for the economic crisis, for what was causing problems in industry; then to see which of these occured in news coverage and which were excluded. Secondly, we examined how some explanations were featured prominently and how others were downgraded.

One of our first detailed studies was of coverage of the car industry. We found ourselves looking mainly at strikes and wage claims. These are not of course the only things that happen in industry, but they are what is called the news. In January 1975 a dispute occurred at British Leyland. This received extensive coverage over a period of five weeks. The association of British Leyland with strikes has now entered the folklore of our society: no football match is complete without a barrier proclaiming that "KENNY (or whoever) STRIKES FASTER THAN LEYLAND". In January 1979 *The Daily Telegraph* reported: "The public in every opinion poll shows that it believes the trade union situation to be more responsible than any other factor for the nation's problems."

We wanted to see how much this view underpinned television
news coverage and how it related it to other possible causes of
the car industry's problems.

What's Wrong With Leyland?

At the time of our study much 'alternative' information on the
car industry was available. This fell into two main areas: low
investment and bad management. British industry as a whole
has suffered from under-investment for at least thirty years. In
the case of the car industry, *The Daily Express* reported in
February 1975 that a Toyota worker in Japan was working
with the equivalent of £11,780 worth of machinery while a
British Leyland worker had only £1,000 worth. There are a
number of reasons for this lack of investment. One is that
capital is being exported from Britain to countries such as
South Africa where profits are higher. Another is that within
the British economy, people with money choose to invest it
where they will receive the highest return. This is often not the
manufacturing industry. For speculative reasons, literally
thousands of millions of pounds have, over the years, been
directed away from production into areas such as the buying up
of property and land. In the period 1974-75 each of the top
three property companies in London had assets greater than
the total value of British Leyland. A third factor is the
distribution of profits as dividends to shareholders.

The Ryder Report on Leyland commissioned by the
government, showed that between 1968 and 1972 the company
had distributed 95% of its profits as dividends. In these years
Leyland had made £74 million in profits; of this only £4 million
was retained for re-investment, while £70 million was
distributed as dividends. Leyland had more obsolete and worn
out machinery than its competitors. The most important
effects of this were that cars cost more per unit to produce and
also that such machinery was likely to break down. In 1975, the
management's own figures showed that they were losing more
through ineffective machinery, and factors such as management errors, than they were losing through strikes at Leyland.
At this time Leyland was a hotch-potch of all the different
parts which had been absorbed into it and different sections
actually produced models which were in competition with each

other. Management and organisational structure were obviously chaotic.

Such explanations conflict with the more common accounts that the problems of industry are caused by strike-prone workers.

"And There Was More Trouble Today" (BBC 1 3.1.75)

On January 3, Harold Wilson, then Prime Minister, made a speech at his Huyton constituency. In it he dealt with the future of government investment in industry and criticised the past record of car production using the words "manifestly avoidable stoppages of production". The precise origin of these stoppages and who was to blame was left ambiguous. Here is the way it was presented on the first BBC bulletin of that night:

> The Prime Minister, in a major speech tonight on the economy, appealed to *management and unions* in the car industry to cut down on what he called "manifestly avoidable stoppages". He said this was especially important now that government money was involved. The decision to help British Leyland was part of the government's fight against unemployment, but the help couldn't be justified if it led to continuing losses. Mr. Wilson singled out for particular blame British Leyland's Austin-Morris division, which he said was responsible last year for a fifth of the stoppages in man days lost of the whole car industry.
>
> (BBC 1 *Early Evening News* 3.1.75)

"The Prime Minister, in a major speech tonight on the economy, appealed to management and unions."

The bulletin continued with filmed extracts of Wilson speaking:

> This is an industry which itself makes a disproportionate contribution to the loss of output through disputes, because with just over 2 per cent of the total employees, 2 per cent of all those working in the whole of Britain, it accounted for one-eighth of all the man days lost in 1974 through disputes and that

was a year, of course, which was inflated by the coal-mining dispute, which we rapidly brought to an end, and it accounted for getting on for one-third of the total national loss through disputes in 1973. *Whether this loss of production was acceptable or not with private capital involved, or whether it was simply that private capital was unable to deal with such problems, is a matter now for historical argument.* What is not a matter for argument for the future, is this: With public capital and an appropriate degree of public ownership and control involved the government could not justify to Parliament or to the taxpayer the subsidising of large factories involving thousands of jobs, factories which could pay their way but are failing to do so because of manifestly avoidable stoppages of production.

(BBC 1 *Early Evening News* 3.1.75)

"The Prime Minister has appealed to workers in the car industry. . ."

There are three points in Wilson's speech which are of interest here. First, the introduction where Wilson is reported as having criticised "management and unions". Second, in all the sections of the speech we are shown, Wilson does not use the word 'strike' but uses the less emotive term 'dispute'. He even rewords well known phrases such as 'the coal-miners' strike' into 'the coal-mining dispute'. Third, he singles out the problems of what he calls "private capital" and notes that "whether this loss of production was acceptable or not with private capital involved, or whether it was simply that private capital was unable to deal with such problems is a matter now for historical argument".

On the same channel an hour and forty-five minutes later, these three things have changed. The speech is now introduced as an appeal to workers alone. It is referred to from now on as a speech about strikes and the sections on the problems of private capital are no longer shown.

> The Prime Minister has appealed *to workers* in the car industry to cut down on avoidable stoppages. He said the industry had a record of strikes out of proportion to its size, and he singled out, for particular blame, British Leyland's Austin-Morris division, which he said was responsible last year for a fifth of the industry's lost production through strikes. Mr. Wilson said that unless labour relations improved, government help for British Leyland would be put in doubt.

The bulletin continued with these extracts from the speech:

> Parts of the British Leyland undertaking are profitable, others are not, but public investment and participation cannot be justified on the basis of continued avoidable loss-making. Our intervention cannot be based on a policy of turning a private liability into a public liability.

> [*BBC cut here*] What is not a matter for argument for the future is this. With public capital and an appropriate degree of public ownership and control involved, the government could not justify to Parliament, or to the taxpayer, the subsidising of large factories which could pay their way, but are failing to do so because of manifestly avoidable stoppages of production.
>
> (BBC 1 *Late News* 3.1.75)

The BBC 2 coverage that evening was still working with the definition of the speech as being about both sides. It was introduced as a "blunt warning to the car industry" and later in the bulletin there was a discussion between an industrial correspondent and the newcaster in which they made it quite clear that the speech was not simply a criticism of the work force.

> NEWSCASTER: Many of the phrases in the Prime Minister's speech are pointed directly at the unions and the labour force, some are pointed at management, like the need for more efficient working methods. Do the management accept that they have got to do some pretty radical rethinking about

production methods and that sort of thing?

(BBC 2 23:16 3.1.75)

This is important as the speech was referred to on a very large number of occasions (44 in all) in conjunction with the coverage of the dispute at Leyland. This was the last time it was referred to as being critical of management.

The ITN coverage at no point acknowledged these criticisms. In the introduction Mr. Wilson was said to have given "workers a blunt warning". In addition to showing excerpts from the speech ITN also had a reporter on the spot who summarised to a camera what he believed it to be about. These summaries again emphasised the speech as an appeal to the workforce:

This was a stern message to come from a Labour Prime Minister, but it was received politely enough by the audience here in a Labour Club in his constituency; but the speech was clearly prompted by the growing number of companies going to the government for help and the large sums of public money involved. Mr. Wilson clearly expects a greater degree of restraint from the *workforce* in firms where the government has stepped in to help and he has appealed directly to *working people* not to rock an already very leaky boat.

(ITN 22:00 3.1.75)

This bulletin continued with reports of attitudes to the speech and to the source of Leyland's difficulties. Elsewhere the alternative history of these difficulties was well documented. The problems of investment and distribution of dividends were in fact highlighted as early as 1972, as for example in this excerpt from the journal *Management Today*:

Capital expenditure had been very low for many years, and depreciation was correspondingly small. The high profits about which so many boasts were made, were thus derived from a declining asset base and too high a proportion was paid out to shareholders.

(*Management Today*, August 1972)

But such alternative accounts were reduced on the news to mere tokens. In the above ITN bulletin, the story on Leyland lasted over five minutes, the first four minutes and 50 seconds of this were taken up with the speech, summaries of it and the definition of it as being about the workforce. The bulletin continued immediately with a *fifteen second* reference to the alternative view. Lesley Huckfield, MP, was quoted as saying that the main problem in Leyland was the management failure to invest. This account was immediately 'sandwiched' by following it with two other views that refuted it, those of the Leyland management and of Mr. Prior, the Conservative spokesman.

Mr. Wilson's comments on British Leyland got a cool reception from one Labour MP, Mr. Leslie Huckfield of Nuneaton. *He said* the Prime Minister clearly knew very little about the car industry, the real cause of the trouble was the chronic failure of management to invest, *he said*. But the opposition's employment spokesman Mr. James Prior, and the British Leyland spokesman, both supported Mr. Wilson's remarks. Mr. Prior said Mr. Wilson was at least stating some home truths which others have been expressing for a long while.

(ITN 22:00 3.1.75)

"He said . . . the real cause was the chronic failure of management to invest."

Huckfield's view is effectively discounted, all the more since it was heavily parenthesised with a double "he said". ITN left us in no doubt as to which side they wished to emphasise. They literally 'underlined' one interpretation of the speech and used this to introduce their coverage of the dispute. The above bulletin continued:

As if to underline Mr. Wilson's remarks, British Leyland's Austin-Morris plant in Cowley announced that 12,000 men are being laid off because of a strike by 250 workers. The striking workers are engine tuners, who want to be graded as skilled workers. They rejected a plea to call off the strike which could cut production by a thousand cars a day.

(ITN *Late News* 3.1.75)

"But the opposition's employment spokesman, Mr. James Prior . . . "

The BBC used the same form of 'sandwich' and also linked the speech and the dispute. We know here that the BBC is about to talk of strikes since it uses the words "and there was more trouble today".

Mr. Wilson's speech has been welcomed by the opposition spokesman on employment, Mr. James Prior. He said the Prime Minister had told car workers some home truths, although it was a pity he hadn't done so before, but Mr. Leslie Huckfield, a Labour MP with a lot of car workers in his constituency of Nuneaton, said the speech was disgraceful. The real culprits were the management, not the workers. British Leyland said tonight they shared Mr. Wilson's exasperation at the series of futile disputes in the corporation *and there was more trouble today.* 12,000 workers at the Cowley plant near Oxford were laid off because of a strike by 250 in the tuning department.

(BBC 1 *Late News* 8.1.75)

This sets the pattern for the subsequent use of the speech in relation to the dispute. It is constantly recalled as the events at Cowley are reported. The apparently routine coverage of a dispute is now underpinned by a series of insertions which point to one interpretation of Leyland's problems.

The last of these references occured seventeen days after the speech was actually made. As the coverage of the dispute moves further away from the actual event of the speech, so the original definition is reworked, always in the direction of blaming the workforce. Wilson's original reference to "manifestly avoidable stoppages" is recalled variously as being about "senseless strikes", "unnecessary strikes" and a warning to "workers in general, but car workers in particular".

The typical pattern is as follows:

... and now they're out again, *within a week in fact of the Prime Minister's warning that what he called unnecessary strikes were putting jobs in the car industry at risk.* And indeed, as a result of this action this morning, 12,000 other British Leyland car workers may well have to be laid off immediately.
(ITN 13:00 9.1.75)

Cowley in Oxford, *specially picked out by Mr. Wilson in his warning last night about strikes,* is at a standstill for a second day because of industrial trouble. 12,000 workers at the plant are being laid off because 250 engine tuners who want to be higher graded are stopping work on Monday. In his speech last night, Mr. Wilson warned workers in general, but car workers in particular, that the government could not justify subsidising large factories which were losing money because of manifestly avoidable strikes. The speech has been welcomed by some Conservative MPs, but condemned by some left-wing Labour members.
(ITN 13:00 4.1.75)

First the fresh strike at British Leyland's. The management at Cowley said this evening that despite the renewed stoppage by the 250 tuners there, they have managed to achieve 80 per cent of a normal day's output. The 12,000 other people who work at Cowley, *the plant which was specifically mentioned by the Prime Minister last week when he talked about senseless strikes in the motor industry* — they were angry this morning when they learned that the tuners had voted to walk out again and that they

faced the threat of layoffs for the second time in four days.
(BBC 2 *Late News* 9.1.75)
Alternative explanations of Leyland's problems are not used
to organise coverage in the same way. For example, two days
after the Wilson speech Jack Jones made a statement criticising
Leyland's management. This was referred to three times on
BBC 1, three times on ITN and not at all on BBC 2. The Jones
statement disappeared very rapidly from the news and
significantly was not used as an organising principle for
coverage. It simply occurs as a fragment which is quickly
passed over. By comparison, the Wilson speech with its new
definition was referred to 13 times on BBC 1, 8 times on BBC 2
and 21 times on ITN.

The definition of Wilson's remarks is used to give authority
for a limited explanation around which the flow of coverage is
being organised. But the view that strikes are the problem has
become so firmly implanted in the normal account of
journalists that at times they feel quite able to embrace it as
their own. For example on January 4 an ITN journalist gave a
report from Cowley and concluded:

The Austin-Morris plant at Cowley is now totally shut down.
Twelve thousand men have been laid off because two hundred
and fifty engine tuners want their jobs regraded. It's the kind of
strike that has contributed significantly to the dire economic
problems of British Leyland.

(ITN 22:00 4.1.75)
While the theme that strikes are the problem is embraced in
this way, there is no point in this five week period of coverage
where any of the other explanations of Leyland's problems are
treated in a similar manner. Journalists never concluded: "it's
the kind of chronic investment failure that has done so much to
contribute to the problems of Leyland."

Information which contradicts the dominant view, if it
appears at all, exists as fragments and is never explored by news
personnel as a rational alternative explanation. It is not used by
them as a way of organising what they cover, of selecting what
they film, or structuring their interviews. Where alternatives
do occasionally surface, as for example when shop stewards are
interviewed, then these accounts are simply fitted into the
dominant flow. This may occur even when the content of such
an interview seriously contradicts the assumptions that the

journalist is pursuing when asking the questions. At Leyland the shop stewards' convenor was interviewed. The reporter set up the interview once again in relation to Wilson's speech, and asked how the men at Cowley were reacting to it. The shop steward convenor argued that this approach did not help, and gave two critical pieces of information that severely contradicted the media view of Leyland. He said that since April of the previous year the men had been working consistently to avoid disputes. The level of disputes in Leyland had in fact fallen in the period to which he was referring. Secondly, he argued that most of the production had been lost through breakdowns or shortages of materials, a point born out by the management's own figures on production losses. Reports confirming the shop steward's view later appeared in four national newspapers, but were never given on the television news.

" .. and tell the viewers, Mr X, when did you stop sleeping on the night shift? "

In this interview the news journalist simply ignores the evidence given to him.

SHOP STEWARDS' CONVENOR: ... Since April of last year, we have worked consistently, all of us, to try and avoid any disputes whatsoever. In fact most of the production that has been lost, has been lost through either breakdowns or shortage of materials and we do recognise that British Leyland has got a problem, a cash-flow problem, and we have worked very, very hard, both union and members, to try and eradicate this position.

BBC REPORTER: How does the prospect of no government cash for British Leyland strike you if the strike record doesn't improve?   (BBC 21:00 6.1.73)

In the face of the evidence that the level of disputes at Leyland has gone down and that anyway most production is not lost through this, the journalist persists with the view that the critical issue is what will happen if the strike record does not improve! It is so much on the tip of his tongue that the journalist (presumably accidentally) actually uses the word 'strike' twice in the same sentence.

Hair-Raising Stories

This treatment of people on the shop floor may be compared with that of *The Financial Times*. Its journalists were sent to Leyland and interviewed shop stewards. On January 6 *The Financial Times* reported: "Cowley shop stewards tell hair-raising stories about managerial failings, and point at the moment to constant assembly-track holdups caused by non-availability of supplier component parts."

Journalists claim in their defence that they play 'devil's advocate' in interviews; that it is their role to present the opposition case and that this provides lively television. Our study showed that they simply did not do this. They do not typically attack the management using the arguments of shop stewards. We can compare the above interview with one in which an ITN journalist interviewed a British Leyland manager. One question does take up briefly the theme of Mr. Jones' criticism of management, the other six speak for themselves:

1. Would workers at Leyland approve of a one-year strike truce?
2. Jones yesterday said management was largely to blame for stoppages — how do you take this?
3. What are stoppages caused by?
4. Isn't this a criticism of the unions as they apparently have so little control over their men?
5. Do you think there are people at work at Leyland who simply want to disrupt the thing?

6.   What danger is there to jobs in Leyland if these sort of strikes go on?

7.   With government coming to the aid of British Leyland, aren't workers going to think their jobs are safe anyway?

(ITN 13:00 6.1.75)

ITN 13:00 6.1.75

BBC1 21:00 6.1.75

We may also note that the shop steward was interviewed with his back to a wall outside the factory gates while the Leyland manager was brought into the comfort and style of the ITN studios for a lengthy face-to-face discussion with the newscaster. What is at stake in all this coverage is the routine processing of information, reports and interviews around one view of industrial crisis. Information that contradicts this is either discounted or ignored and at times is actually used as if it supports the dominant view. In one instance, government figures were released showing that overall car sales were down. The main cause of this was the oil crisis and the increasing cost of fuel. Television programmes showed fields which were full of cars that could not be sold. These were cars that had been completed and had left the factory. They were unlikely, therefore, to be affected by strikes. Logically if there were less strikes there would be even more cars which would not be sold. Yet an ITN news actually ran the story of the unsold cars directly in conjunction with the alleged strike problem at Leyland.

". . . a calamity if the strike situation there gets worse. Figures show . . ."

On the day that it has been announced by the Government that new car sales last year were down by 25 per cent on 1973, *the Director of British Leyland's Cowley plant has warned of a calamity if the strike situation there gets worse. Figures out today*

show that private car and van registrations dropped from
1,688,000 in 1973 to 1,273,000 last year and all vehicle
registrations were down nearly as much by 20 per cent. The
warning came in a letter from the Plant Director, Mr. John
Symons, to Leyland employees as the Company and the
Engineering Union agreed to talks tomorrow at the
Conciliation and Arbitration Service to try to solve the strike of
engine tuners at Cowley. Mr.Symons said that the strike had
meant that Cowley was failing to meet what he called its survival
budget. He also gave a warning that a further deterioration
would be calamitous with the strongest likelihood of a major
reduction in manufacturing and employment at Cowley.

(ITN 22:00 22.1.75)

The news is one-dimensional in that it pursues one
explanation at the expense of others. A count of the causes of
Leyland's problems which were referred to in the Cowley
coverage gives some indication of this. *Excluding* all of the
references to Wilson's speech they were as follows. On BBC 1
there were 22 references to the strike problem of Leyland, 5
references to the problem of management, and only one to
investment. On BBC 2 there were 8 references to the strike
theme, 3 to management and 2 to investment. On ITN there
were 33 to the strike theme, 8 to management and none to
investment. Such a count actually over-estimates the presence
of alternative explanations since these occur only as fragments
and are never pursued. By contrast the strike theme runs
through the coverage of the car industry. The news is
organised around the logic of this explanation. When strikes
are presented as a source of industry's problems we know and
are informed exactly of what strikes do. The resources of the
media are organised to give us this information. A kind of chain
of information is set up by which we know what a strike is,
what it does, who it affects, the damage it causes and who is to
blame. We are routinely told who is on strike, who is
responsible, who is left-wing, if there are splits in the unions
and how many exports are lost. When themes such as left-wing
influence and deliberate wrecking are inserted they create the
links in how we are to understand what is happening. Such
insertions may occur quite gratuitously, even when there is no
immediate story. In this sense, to be on the news you do not
have to do anything 'newsworthy' at all. For a left-wing shop

steward, complete non-actions are sufficient to have a personal history of months ago once more regurgitated. In this piece of ITN news, also 'unavailable for comment' was Mr. Alan Thornett:

Other officials refused to comment at all. These included district secretary Mr. Malcolm Young and shop steward Mr. Alan Thornett. He was the man at the centre of last summer's strike when Leyland sought to have him removed from union office, because they claimed he was seeking deliberately to disrupt production.

(ITN 22:00 6.1.75)

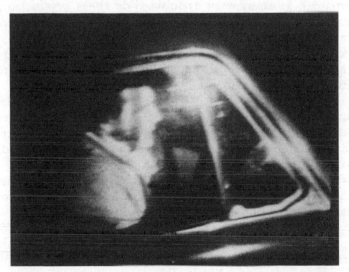

"Other officials refused to comment at all. These included . . . the man at the centre of last summer's strike . . . "

Similarly the view that strikes are the problem becomes so routinised that it may occur even when the immediate subject does not call for it, as for example in the description of a new Leyland car which was about to be launched:

Onlookers outside the Cowley factory gates have been getting an unplanned preview of a new British Leyland car. It's the successor to the Austin 1800 range, code-named 8071 and due to be launched in spring, *strikes permitting*. British Leyland hope it will revive interest in their cars in a sagging home market.

(BBC 1 21:00 9.1.75)

The news is underpinned by a key ideological assumption. It is that production in our society is normal and satisfactory unless there are problems with the workforce. All of the other problems which may be generated by a productive system based on private interest — such as the export of capital and the flow of investment funds away from manufacturing, the running down of some sections of the economy and the rapid expansion of others, the need to keep shareholders happy, and to distribute dividends — are closed off in the flow of coverage. Although these factors are clearly responsible for major disruptions in the economy they remain unexamined by journalists as sources of trouble. For them production is normal until there is a dispute. As for example in this coverage from ITN:

> For a week now the company has been keeping production up to eighty per cent of normal and stockpiling cars for the tuners to attend to when the dispute is settled.
>
> (ITN 13:00 20.1.75)

What is crucial is that normal production and full production are treated as synonymous and are equated with being strike free. In the coverage of the above dispute ITN informed us that:

> With the engine tuners back at work at least for the time being, the Austin-Morris plant, singled out by the Prime Minister for particular criticism, *was also back in full production.*
>
> (ITN 13:00 7.1.75)

A production stoppage or a problem in industry becomes equated in general usage with a strike. This occurs across industrial reporting. Here, for example, in coverage of Chrysler, a reporter notes that stocks must be good because there have been no strikes:

> With a touch of irony, Chrysler point out that they'd had a run *without production stoppages, without strikes,* so stocks must be good, but for all their optimism their workforce is going on a three day week for the rest of January.
>
> (BBC 1 21:00 9.1.75)

The journalists view of the 'normal' covers up the nature of a system which through its own logic can produce chaos and decline, independent of the wishes or actions of the workforce — but it is at their door that the blame is laid.

Leyland Again — Déjà Vu

In February 1979 we took an additional sample of coverage of a Leyland dispute to compare with earlier results. For two weeks, we recorded the main evening bulletin on BBC 1 and ITN and the Sunday evening News Review on BBC 2. On February 7 the workers at the Longbridge plant in Birmingham came out on unofficial strike. They said they were protesting at management's refusal to make back-dated parity payments which had been agreed by both sides in return for higher levels of productivity. In the context of the agreement the unions had conceded that redundancies could take place. The shop stewards pointed out that 7000 redundancies had occurred and claimed that management were attempting to conceal the true levels of production at both Austin-Morris and Jaguar. Management claimed that productivity had not been high enough to justify the payments, that the men had misunderstood the terms of the agreement and that the shop stewards were breaking procedure.

Given that management and unions had competing explanations to offer for the dispute, in principle each of these might have been explored in an even-handed way. In the main however, coherence and rationality are granted to management and not to the workforce. The different ways in which both groups are interviewed reflects this. It is not enough to analyse formal balance in terms of the time allocated to the two groups (in this case the workers and their representatives had more than management). The style of the interview also matters. Questions put to management tend either to be an open invitation to give their views or to lead directly to these. As a result such interviews are fairly harmonious: the 'devil's advocate' role and the 'difficult' questions are reserved largely for shop stewards.

Interviews with Pat Lowry (personnel director of B.L. cars) and Ray Horrocks (managing director, Austin-Morris) began with an open invitation to them to elaborate upon their views. These were allowed to stand without interruption or challenge. On the rare occasions when a second question was put to them, it was encouraging rather than challenging. Thus on BBC 1, a journalist interviews Horrocks:

JOURNALIST: ... when I spoke to the boss of Austin-Morris,

of which Longbridge is the biggest part, I asked him if the
workers had been deliberately misled by the stewards.

HORROCKS: I am saying they were given wrong information
without any shadow of a doubt at all and that is now very
evident. Because against the background of the same
information, 66,000 workers in 27 plants right across the
country have voted to stay at work.

JOURNALIST: So what's the message in that for Longbridge?

(BBC 1 21:00 7.2.79)

And on ITN:

JOURNALIST: If Longbridge doesn't go back, Leyland say other plants are going to be hit. And there is a long term threat too.

HORROCKS: In what I think is the unlikely event that Longbridge stay out — there's no doubt at all in my mind, I shall have to ask the Chief Executive of B.L. Ltd. that I should reappraise the Austin-Morris plant, and that will have long-term implications for the Company.

JOURNALIST: What sort of implications?

(ITN 22:00 7.2.79)

The aggressive questions put to shop stewards and pickets stand out in marked contrast. Here, for example, a BBC journalist interviews the Longbridge convenor of shop stewards:

JOURNALIST: The vote was in favour of an instant walk-out. There have been dire warnings that another stoppage could spell the end of British Leyland. After this one would there be a plant or a job to come back to?

SHOP STEWARD: I'm confident we shall have a plant and a job to go back to. I note that Mr. Edwards might not have a job. Indeed, he's already seeking tax exile. I wish that some of our members on the wages that we get could seek tax exile, at the same rate as himself.

JOURNALIST: *Leyland workers over recent years have got a reputation with the public for perhaps doing things very quickly and doing sometimes stupid things* — is this one of them?

SHOP STEWARD: I wouldn't have thought so. But you know, you were here last year when we persuaded our members not to. If anyone's adopted a responsible attitude it's the workers at Longbridge.

JOURNALIST: *Was it responsible to go ahead with this strike?*

(BBC 1 21:00 7.2.79)

And on ITN:

JOURNALIST: There were clashes this morning between pickets and drivers trying to get building materials through to a plant that will build the new Mini — the car that is the key to the Company's future. *Aren't the men cutting their own throats?*

SHOP STEWARD: We're on strike. It's been forced upon us. We've got no alternative. And we intend to use the full force of our membership in picketing this plant to ensure that nothing

moves in and nothing moves out. We regret that we have to do
these things. But until such time as the management come down
to earth, that's how it will continue.
JOURNALIST: *Even if it destroys the Company?*
                                        (ITN 22:00 8.2.79)
Management or official views tend to form the basis of such
news accounts. At times, they are embellished to give them
maximum emphasis, as in this report by a BBC correspondent:
"B.L. management wasn't slow to *blast back* at the Longbridge
stewards for acting unconstitutionally, breaking procedure,
overturning the secret ballot vote and spreading inaccurate
information." He refers to output and productivity figures
and tells us: "Now the extra productivity is measured against
output in 1977 — *goodness knows, a bad year for disputes . . .*"
The report ends with the declaration:

> An all-out strike could mean B.L. revising the corporate plan it
> has submitted to the NEB, cutting back investment, cutting
> back jobs. The failure of British car companies to produce cars
> means a boost for imports which, we learn, accounted for 54% of
> all sales last month, when *incidentally*, B.L. cars were market
> leader for the fourth consecutive month.

Management are not typically challenged and they emerge as
victims — having to revise the corporate plan, cut jobs and
investment because of the strike. There is no longer any room
for a logical alternative view. The last phrase — "B.L. cars were
market leader for the fourth consecutive month" — is literally
treated as incidental information. It could within an
alternative frame have been used to contradict or at least
challenge the conventional view that B.L. is failing to produce
cars because of frequent strikes.

The effect of all this is to produce a critical distinction
between responsible citizens and those few individuals or
unions who are rocking the boat. The solid consensus of right-
thinking, decent, law-abiding, hard-working taxpayers is
compared with the wild, irresponsible minority. At its crudest,
this is presented as the unions on one side and the taxpayer on
the other. On February 8, 1979, ITN opened its main news
with the headline:
LEYLAND UNIONS SAY: LET THE TAXPAYERS PAY.
This was a factually incorrect report of the unions' views. At
the time Leyland was desperately short of capital. The chief

negotiator of the unions recalls to us that he told a reporter that Leyland would be a good investment for the National Enterprise Board. The state already owned most of the assets of Leyland and had lent it money. But on such loans up to $15\frac{1}{2}\%$ was being charged in interest — the taxpayer was not *giving* anything. More importantly, such a statement misses the issues of *who* are the taxpayers, and what are their real interests. At this time over half a million people were employed directly or indirectly by Leyland. They paid about £750 million in tax a year, which is very much more than the state lends to Leyland. It is absurd to imply that Leyland workers are different from other taxpayers and even more absurd to suggest that taxpayers as a whole would be better off if Leyland collapsed. The effect on the economy would be, at the least, to put an enormous number of people out of work, given all the industries that depend upon car production. Unemployment pay would then have to be met by those that are still paying tax.

Such headlines are no more than crude ideology. The blaming of the unions on the one side and the championing of the 'taxpayer' on the other lays the foundations for the most conservative economic policies. It plays right into the hands of monetarism — the belief that market forces should be unleashed for a competition in which only the strong survive. In this bleak vision the state should no longer intervene to hold back unemployment and recession. Instead, these should be allowed to develop so that wages will be forced down to the benefit of those who employ labour. Television has done much to make this scenario possible. Working people are presented as having brought unemployment upon themselves. The taxpayers, those that are left, can rest easily.

III

"REASONABLE MEN AND RESPONSIBLE CITIZENS"

Economic Coverage

Just as the coverage of industry is organised around limited and conservative explanations, so is news on the economy as a whole. In this case we show how television news was organised around an account which blamed inflation mainly on wages and then linked this explanation to the political policy of wage restraint. Here again what underpins media coverage is scrutiny of working people rather than an analysis of 'normal' operations of the economy and its ability to generate crisis.

Sky High Prices

The key problem underlying Britain's economic decline is the failure of industrial investment. On rare occasions this has been acknowledged even on the television news. In January 1975 the industrial editor of ITN made the following reference: "Since the war, Britain's overriding problem, almost universally agreed, has been a failure to invest adequately." (ITN 22:00 21.1.75). We have already shown how this affected particular industries such as cars. In fact the decline of investment was widespread across the whole of the manufacturing sector. Between 1960 and 1972 Britain re-invested 16-18% of its gross national product each year. By comparison Japan was investing 30-35%, almost twice the rate.*

*Figures from D. Yaffe, 'The Crisis of Profitability', *New Left Review* 80, 1973.

In some areas the difference was staggering. While in 1978
Mr.Callaghan was announcing a government grant at around
£100 million for the computer industry, the Japanese
government and industrial interests were going ahead with the
injection of £35,000 **million** into theirs.* The main reason for
the long term decline of manufacturing investment in Britain
has been simply that profit returns from it have been low.

Consequently those with capital have invested in other areas.
This had the effect of lowering productivity relative to
Britain's competitors, and also fuelled inflation as the money
found other purposes. For example, *The Investor's Chronicle*
here describes the effect on prices when the property boom
began to take off:

*C. Evans, *The Mighty Micro*, Victor Gollancz, London, 1979, p.93.

In the summer of 1973, the government was allowing the amount of money for use in the country to expand rapidly in the hope that industry would use it to invest in new plant to produce more goods and earn more foreign exchange by exporting.

It did not work out that way, because industry was not confident that it could sell enough goods profitably enough to cover the money for new plant. So the extra money being pumped into the economy found other uses.

At first some of it found its way into buying shares where it helped to force prices up. More important, vast amounts of money were being lent by the banking system to buy property. Since property is in limited supply, the main effect was to force prices sky high.†

The relative fall in investment had another disastrous consequence: it raised the serious prospect of major unemployment. Since the Second World War all Western governments had been committed to maintaining high levels of employment and to intervening in the economy to ensure that there was no return to the slump of the thirties. Capitalism was not to be abolished either by Labour or Conservative policies, but it could be modified in the name of producing social harmony. In effect what happened was that successive governments were forced to step in either to buy up the bankrupt sections of manufacturing industry or to prop up the weak sections with grants and loans. This, together with regional aid grants and indirect subsidies to industry, such as expenditure on motorways, had a major effect on government spending. In May 1975, *The Observer* reported that public borrowing by the government had quadrupled in just over one year to £10,000 million. In effect the government was making up for the failures of private investment. The problem was that in doing this, it was spending more on this and in other areas such as welfare spending, than it was raising through taxation. This was a major factor in the development of inflation, since the government was effectively printing the extra money. A critical problem by the mid-1970s was how to claw this money back out of the economy. The three chosen solutions were to increase taxation, cut 'unnecessary' spending on areas such as hospitals and schools, and hold down wages. At the time of our

†*The Investor's Chronicle*, Editorial, 11 September, 1974.

study in 1975, wage restraint was very much in the air and political figures such as Denis Healey were arguing that wages had caused inflation as a way of justifying these policies. This view was espoused by most of the right and centre of the Labour Party. The unions did not in general agree that they had caused inflation and the TUC was divided over whether or not wage restraint was an acceptable way to reduce it.

The argument that wages had caused price increases was a dubious one. It hinged on the view that wages were shooting ahead and somehow dragging prices along behind them. In fact in the whole period 1970-75 real wages had remained about the same and for the first six months of 1975 had actually fallen. In any case prices do not have to rise simply because wages do. If sufficient investment is undertaken, then productivity can increase and manufacturers can afford to increase wages and in some cases may even lower the cost of the product. Workers in countries such as Germany and France, where there are higher levels of investment, receive higher wages, yet the rate of inflation there is lower than in Britain.

The view that wages were responsible for the crisis was rejected by large sections of the trade unions, and was also criticised from the right. Monetarists in the Conservative Party blamed inflation on excessive state spending. Obviously they did not relate this spending to a general theory of capitalist crisis. They saw the decline as coming from 'subsidised incompetence', 'lazy workers' and 'lack of initiative'. They were against subsidising weak sections of industry and saw the solution as allowing the economy to move into a slump. In this situation unemployment would force wages down and the new conditions would hopefully be taken advantage of by the owners of capital who survived the crisis. Although these policies were clearly not designed to help working people, it is the case that the theory behind them definitely implied that wages were not the initial cause of inflation. This was stated quite openly by monetarists at the Conservative Party Conference of October 1976. The policies of wage restraint were denounced as a 'con-trick' on these grounds. As early as January 1974 Nicholas Ridley (Under-Secretary for Trade and Industry in Edward Heath's Conservative government) wrote:

Contrary to the popular view, the cause of inflation is not high wage settlements but the way in which they are financed. In the public sector, wages must be paid for out of the earnings of the firm. If this is done, no inflation results. It is only when the Government pays for high public sector wage settlements or receives bankrupt companies with money that it prints, that inflation results.

(The Sunday Times, 20.1.74)

There were other arguments about what had contributed to inflation, such as the effects of oil price increases. Most economists are agreed that this had some effect, but it cannot really explain Britain's economic problems since the oil crisis affected all Western countries in much the same way. Yet Britain's inflation rate was much higher than most.

Rampant Wages?

There were three main positions on what had caused the economic crisis and inflation, but only one of these directly blamed wages. Yet the news consistently pursued the theme that wages were the cause of inflation. Our study on the first four months of 1975 showed that on the news, statements saying that wages were the main cause outnumbered by eight to one those reports which rejected this view. The argument that wages were the problem was linked by news journalists to political policies such as the need for wage restraint. For example, the industrial correspondent of the BBC commented in January 1975:

With wages now as the main boost in inflation, just getting inflation down to a reasonable level seems to imply tougher pay restraint.

(BBC 1 21:00 20.1.75)

In this period there were 17 occasions when views were given on the news that the policies of wage restraint and lower wages were *not* the best way to solve the economic crisis. There were 287 occasions when the view was featured that these were exactly what *was* needed.

As we showed in the case of the car industry, the importance of these references is not so much how many times they appear, but that they are used to organise coverage around limited explanations. Here again, the alternatives, where they appear, are mere fragments, while the dominant theme of wage

inflation and the need for restraint is at the core of news
gathering and reporting. The link between wages and prices
was simply assumed in a series of discussions and reports.
Month after month on the news we were shown graphs and
charts to illustrate how much wages and prices had gone up.
The link is a dubious one since, of course, many factors can
cause price increases apart from wages. The conclusion of all
these reports was that wages were ahead of prices. For example,
BBC 1 informed us in one bulletin in January 1975 that "wage

inflation is still accelerating sharply with earnings keeping well ahead of prices" — that "average earnings also soared" and that they were "far outstripping the retail price increases". Such coverage was typical over the first four months of 1975. Its conclusions are even more dubious since it is not clear that wages were in fact ahead of prices at this time. In a study of real income published in 1976, Frances Cairncross concluded that "the purchasing power of the average male worker's earnings has been virtually unchanged for four years".

Unreliable Guides

One reason why wage rises constantly appeared on the news as if they were ahead of prices was that the official figures on these were often reported without important qualifications. These included at the very minimum the need to allow for tax and other deductions to indicate the real value of wage increases. Without these qualifications wages could be made to look as if they were "outstripping" prices. In the case of ITN on 11 occasions when they gave the figures, 6 made no reference to what *real* wages were. For the BBC the gross figures were given without reference to real wages on 17 occasions out of a total of 20 in their reports on wages and prices figures. The difference is clear if we compare a report which includes the qualifications and one from which they have been dropped. In its early evening news report on January 20 the BBC reported:

> Meanwhile the nation's wage bill is going up faster than ever before. Official figures today show that average earnings last November were 25 per cent higher than in the same month in 1973, a record increase. Our economics correspondent says that *after taxation, the actual rise in spending power is just over 20 per cent*. That is still ahead of the increase in retail prices of 18.3 per cent.
>
> (BBC 1 17:45 20.1.75)

On the same channel three hours later, the qualifications have been dropped:

> NEWSCASTER: The figures published today by the Department of Employment show that wage inflation is still accelerating sharply, with earnings keeping well ahead of prices. During 1974 basic weekly wage rates rose by a record 28½ pence in the pound. While in the year up to last November, *average*

earnings, which include overtime and bonus pay, *also soared by a record 25.3 per cent, far outstripping the retail price increases* of 18 per cent during the same period.

(BBC 1 21:00 20.1.75)

Indeed the BBC became so wedded to the view that wages were far ahead of prices that at one point it actually altered the normal way in which these figures are reported, to draw the conclusion more firmly. The usual way of measuring increases in pay is the index of average earnings. Both channels have acknowledged that this is the most reliable guide; for example, a BBC correspondent noted on 19 February 1975 that "it is the best guide that there is to the relationship between pay and prices." (BBC 1 17:45 19.2.75). Similarly ITN in comparing wages and prices figures had concluded: "This is the comparison which really counts, the *average earnings* of seven million workers." (ITN 22:00 20.1.75).

"This is the comparison which really counts, the average earnings . . . "

There is another index of wages called the index of basic weekly wage rates. This can be unreliable since it measures only what the basic rate is supposed to be. If, for example, people are on short-time because of recession, then the figures will over-estimate what people are receiving. This is exactly what was happening by April of 1975. Yet the BBC main news introduced the wages and prices figures for that month as follows:

> Well, these figures rub in Mr.Healey's warnings about wage-led inflation, and pay rises well in excess of the cost of living. And they reveal a widening disparity between pay and prices. The percentage increase in *basic weekly wage rates* for the year to March is 32.5 per cent against an increase of 19.9 per cent in the latest retail price index in the twelve months to February.
>
> (BBC 1 21:00 16.4.75)

"These figures rub in Mr. Healey's warnings . . . The percentage increase in basic weekly wage rates . . ."

Of the six BBC bulletins which discussed these figures (on 16, 18 and 20 April) only two mentioned even briefly the index of average earnings. The average earnings index showed that falling industrial output was holding back the rise in real income. *The Times* in fact commented on the day after the above BBC bulletin:

> There is accumulating evidence that falling industrial output and the increase in short-time working is beginning to hold back the rise in actual earnings, which include payments for overtime and bonuses.
>
> (*The Times*, 17.4.75)

Figures and information on the economy were thus organised to lay the blame for inflation on wages. The above

example shows how this account was then used to 'rub in' the
views of Healey.

Rubbing in Mr. Healey's Warnings

We are obviously not complaining here about the presence of
Mr. Healey on the screen. It would be naive to imagine that a
national television service could or should avoid reporting the
views of the Chancellor. Our criticism is that the resources of
the media were used to underline, develop and give legitimacy
to these views. They provide the logic around which coverage
is organised — they are embraced by the journalists and are
constantly reiterated and given credence by being linked with
apparently incontrovertible information. For example in the
BBC coverage of March 1975 a speech by Healey on the 'lunacy
of wage increases' is linked to *unqualified* figures on wages and
prices.

> NEWSCASTER: From the Chancellor of the Exchequer,
> Mr.Denis Healey, *a stern warning* on the effect of wage inflation.
> The Chancellor told a meeting of the Parliamentary Labour
> Party this morning that *to ignore current wage rises was
> irresponsible lunacy.* At the same time official figures were

BBC 2 17:45 19.3.75

published showing that wages are now about 29% higher than a
year ago while prices have risen by 10% less. Here's our
economics correspondent . . .
ECONOMICS CORRESPONDENT: The gap between wages
and prices is one of Mr. Healey's big problems as he plans his
budget. He said this morning wage settlements were just not
close enough to the social contract guidelines and were
responsible for the worst rise in prices.

(BBC 1 17:45 19.3.75)

The report is consistently from the point of view of Mr.
Healey. Journalists feel quite able to underline what he knows
and doesn't know. Later in the same report we are told:

Last year wages did keep ahead of prices and current wages are
also doing so, for thousands of workers in many trades, getting
rises of 35 and 40% above a year ago. *Mr. Healey knows this can't
go on.*

"Mr. Healey knows this can't go on."

It might be noted that thousands of workers were not receiving
such increases. *The Times* reported in August of that year that
average earnings in the first six months of 1975 had *fallen* in
real terms by 10%. In the above bulletins the correspondent's
claims on the effects of wages were followed by further
references to what Mr. Healey wanted. After these is what
amounts to a throw-away line referring to alternative views on
the economy:

③ He (Mr. Healey) wants more modest wage deals and better output per man. Without it he forecasts prices will be rising twice as fast in Britain as in those countries competing with us. The message from the Chancellor called for belt-tightening *and the party meeting rejected a call from the left-wing Tribune group for an opposite give-away budget.* This afternoon MPs were gloomily forecasting higher income tax ...

(BBC 1 17:45 19.4.75)

A whole tradition of Keynesian economics is here reduced to a call for an "opposite give-away budget". There are no reports or information included to make sense of, or to underline, the *Tribune* view. What there is here is an illusion of balance, whereby statements are included from what appear as different sides. But the reported views have a totally different status, legitimacy and meaning in the text. Only one set 'makes sense' in that we are systematically given the information necessary to understand the explanations and policies to which they relate. When the budget did appear a month later, it was presented on the news as if it were a necessary response to the inflation that had allegedly been caused by trade union activity. On ITN for example, it was introduced as follows:

Good evening. In the toughest of budgets the Chancellor, *Mr.*

"Mr. Healey has fired a broadside at all those who have taken high pay rises."

*Healey, has fired a broadside at all those who have taken high pay
rises.* These, he said, were the main cause of the present rate of
inflation.
                                              (ITN 22:00 15.4.75)
We may ask who were "all those who had taken high pay rises".
ITN had reported in the previous month that according to the
government, 75% of all pay rises were being settled within the
social contract. Most of these workers had in effect taken wage
cuts.
    The effects of the budget of that year were in fact heavily
deflationary. It increased taxation and was designed to claw
back money out of the economy. This was a bitterly
controversial move: the unions predicted that it would
massively increase unemployment. A justification and
rationale for the budget were thus essential for the
government. A series of reports was released from official
sources, such as the Bank of England and the Price
Commission, and these were used in the media to underline the
necessity of the Government's position. The report from the
Price Commission appeared shortly after the April budget at a
critical moment in the arguments. This was covered
intensively on both channels. The message on wages and
inflation was clear:

NEWSCASTER: And now the economy. Prices in Britain rose at
their fastest rate ever between December and February, *mainly
due to high wage settlements,* according to the Price Commission
report published today. In three months up to last December,
the Commission approved an average of £350 million in price
increases each month, particularly in nationalised industries, but
as subsidies started to be phased out and *the big pay increases
started to push labour costs higher,* the Commission were forced
to allow an average of £1,105 million in increases each month
between December and February. This quarterly figure is about
as large as the previous nine months combined. Well, here with a
report is our industrial correspondent, Giles Smith.

GILES SMITH: Today's message from the Price Commission is
grim and it's no less grim because it's not a new one. Inflation is
now rampant and, according to the Commission, *wage inflation
is almost entirely to blame.* Ominously, they say the pace of the
prices explosion has so far been understated. In the three
months covered, the retail prices index went up 5.8 per cent,

wholesale prices 6.5 per cent, but the Commission's own index, which should be more up to date, rose 7.5 per cent. For this *the Commission firmly blame wage-cost increases.*

(ITN 22:00 29.4.75)

"According to the Commission, wage inflation is almost entirely to blame."

ITN reported the Commission as saying that wages were "almost entirely" to blame for inflation. The BBC that night actually put a figure on the precise effect of wages. They reported that "between 60 and 75 pence in the pound" of all price increases came from wages. Such a heavy and unqualified repetition of the theme of wage inflation seemed extraordinary, given the alternative evidence that real wages (for most workers) were probably falling. When we examined the actual document that the Price Commission published it was apparent that it blamed inflation on a range of factors, including, for example, the increases in oil prices. It had estimated the precise effect of each factor on price increases. The Commission had calculated that the direct contribution of labour costs to price increases was only 20%. Yet both ITN and the BBC reported the effect of wages as massively above this. We were curious to see how this disparity had occurred. The reason was that the Price Commission had estimated upwards its own figures for the effect of wage costs on prices.

According to a report in *The Financial Times* the following day, it had done this in two ways. Firstly, in its revised figures, the Commission had *removed* the effects of oil from the calculation and this had put the contribution of wages up from 20% to 30%. Secondly, they introduced the concept of 'indirect wages', on the grounds that everything, even raw materials involved a wage element.

Of course such a very general conception makes the precise calculation of exactly what is happening to wages very difficult if not impossible. Nonetheless the Price Commission concluded that the effect of 'indirect wages' could be calculated by multiplying the figure for the direct effect of wages by "probably two to two and a half times". The BBC had presumably arrived at its own figures by multiplying the figure of 30% (which was wages after removing oil) by two to two and a half. Whatever the logic of all these calculations they become simply absurd mathematically at this point. Percentages cannot be multiplied by fixed amounts in this way. Both BBC and ITN were in grave danger of having more percentages than would fit into a hundred. They had given such high figures for the effect of wages that all the other factors could no longer be fitted in. The logic of the report was that well over a hundred per cent of all price increases now came from wages, oil, and all the other factors.

These figures were indeed attacked the next day in the press — from both right and left. *The Daily Telegraph* argued from a monetarist position that wage increases "are not themselves the cause of inflation" and blamed the problem on the government printing money. *The Morning Star* attacked the calculations in detail and argued that the Price Commission had used "highly dubious arithmetic and reasoning".

Given the history and established traditions of the television news it would be naive to think that journalists would be allowed to attack such an 'authoritative' source as a government commission. It would be inconceivable to imagine the news beginning with: "Good evening, with highly dubious arithmetic and reasoning the Price Commission has claimed tonight that wages are almost entirely to blame for inflation." Yet by the standards of impartiality and neutrality which broadcasters lay claim to, the reporting of such documents is totally inadequate. In the case of the Price Commission report

at no point in any of the bulletins was there a comment on how
the high figures for the effect of wages had been arrived at, and
at no point is the information given that the proven figure for
the effect of wages was only 20%. This figure in fact
represented a *decline* in the effect of wages on the previous
quarter, which was again not reported on the news. On both
BBC and ITN the highest possible estimate of the effect of
wages on inflation was taken. The media here are not merely
reporting the views of important people, but are actually
developing them. The journalists feel able to step into the
minds of senior civil servants and tell us what they are thinking
or who is to blame. The above report on the Price Commission
was followed on ITN by a list of the culprits:

"As the Commission Chairman, Sir Arthur Cockfield, states ... "

As the Commission Chairman, Sir Arthur Cockfield, states,
"taking industry as a whole, the primary factor causing wages to
rise is and can only be rising labour costs." *Well the sort of wage
rises the Commission is thinking about are* those in the 30 per cent
plus bracket and today there came another: the 11,000 London
dockers who were on strike for 5 weeks just a while ago were
today offered and accepted a pay deal which averages out at well
over 30 per cent. On the face of it well outside the Social
Contract guidelines. Tonight, too, a new threat from the

electricity power engineers to strike in support of a 33 per cent pay claim.

(ITN 22:00 29.4.75)

"The 11,000 London dockers who were on strike . . . "

The shots of the dockers at a mass meeting function simply as 'wallpaper' over which the commentary about their pay award is read. No docker is asked to comment on the views of the Price Commission. The 'authoritative' source takes precedence, and the shots of the meeting stand in sharp contrast to the picture of the Commission Chairman and the high status which is given to his words.

The content of the news is organised in such a way that coherence is given to only one set of explanations and policies. What we are indicating here is not isolated pieces of 'bias'. The problem is much more profound than this. The logic of one group of explanations is built into the text. This logic dictates the flow of information, the range of accounts and the legitimacy that is given to these. In the case of economic news, the premise that wage increases have caused inflation and the economic crisis is followed through to the conclusion that wage restraint and higher taxation are necessary. This item from BBC 2 *News Review* summarises this position:

Now home, and as you know this week there's been a lot of heavy news on the country's economic front. Two figures from the week give the real story. Everything else in one way or another is reaction to those figures. One: prices rose in the last twelve months by the biggest ever increase, 21 per cent. Two: wages rose in the last twelve months by a far greater figure, 32 per cent. The Chancellor for one regards that extra 11 per cent on wages as the main cause of inflation. His answer, as we saw in the budget on Tuesday, is to take the extra money away in taxes.

(BBC 2 18:15 20.4.75)

A synthesis is thus made between a restricted and narrow economic explanation and the political policies that apparently flow from it. When this economic view is pursued the logic of who is to blame is inescapable. It seems perfectly natural to monitor wage claims, rather than the actions of those who own capital. This becomes so routine that journalists could dispense with apparently emotive terms such as 'excessive'. They have only to say, "and tonight another wage claim", for everyone to know what they mean and at whom the finger is being pointed.

In fact journalists do sometimes use emotive terms and make their attitudes to trade unions quite clear. In the following interview, an ITN newscaster asks a trade unionist from the National Union of Bank Employees about their wage claims:

INTERVIEWEE: Our job as a trade union is to maintain the purchasing power of our members' salaries and that's all we're trying to do with the pay claim that we've now formulated.

ITN PRESENTER: But as *reasonable men and responsible citizens* can you say that's all you are trying to do and all you are interested in when you hear warnings from the Chancellor to the effect that increases of this sort are going to wreck the national economy?

(ITN 13:00 24.2.75)

Two months later the same newscaster is pursuing the same theme — this time with the General Secretary of the train drivers' union:

Can we look at your claim you've already got in; you see, I mean, you said to one of my colleagues not long ago on this programme that this claim was likely then — this was in February — to be in the range of 25 per cent to 30 per cent; now, you see, that is already between 5 per cent and 10 per cent more than the rise in prices *and it's just this excessive demand above the price rise that Mr. Healey was saying was endangering our whole national*

economy.
                                        (ITN 13:00 16.4.75)
Wage claims in the period which we studied were carefully
monitored and examined on the news to see whether they were
acceptable on the terms that were being set by the government
— whether they were inside or outside the social contract. The
most dire warnings interpenetrate such reports of wage claims.
In this example we are unable to hear what the miners are doing
without being told what Mr. Healey would think about it:
   The Chancellor of the Exchequer, *Mr. Healey, has warned again*
   of excessive wage increases as the miners start negotiating on their
   claim for up to 43 per cent. Mr. Healey said in London tonight
   that Britain could be bankrupt if the national wage bill were too
   high this year — but it needn't happen if the workers stuck
   strictly to the Social Contract. During the day the Coal Board
   twice increased their offer to the miners, mainly to the benefit of
   those working underground.
                                        (BBC 1 21:00 11.2.75)
The monitoring of pay claims and their 'acceptability' was
consistently from the Healey point of view. At the time of our
study the Social Contract was supposed to mean that wages
should go up by about as much as the cost of living. In other
words wages should not rise in real terms, but neither should
they fall. But on the television news the Social Contract was
deemed to have been broken *only* in the sense that workers
were thought to have received 'too much'. There were cases in
this period in which working people took wage settlements
which could not possibly have kept up with the cost of living —
which were in fact wage cuts. These were reported merely as
being 'inside' the Social Contract. There were no fears
expressed by television journalists on these occasions and no
Chancellors were questioned on the breaking of acts of faith.
   In subsequent years it became impossible to sustain this
impression of wages soaring above prices. Living standards
began to fall quite dramatically in many employment sectors.
An analysis of the four years after 1975 demonstrates this, even
if wages are taken in gross terms. In real terms, living standards
fell between January 1975 and January 1977 by approximately
10 per cent. A study by us in 1979 showed that by then, wages
and prices figures were being reported quite differently. They
were still reported, but *separately* — without comparison. For

example, the BBC reported on 14 February that the latest
figures from the Department of Employment meant that most
settlements were "around 10 per cent". Two days later, the
same programme (BBC 1's *Nine O'Clock News*) carried a
report on prices which said that "inflation could be back in
double figures by early summer". The BBC did *not* report that
for the low paid, the inflation rate would be even higher than
the official figure suggested, since the cost of basic essentials
such as food tends to rise faster than the general level of prices.
Nor did the BBC point out that by the time tax was paid on the
new wage settlements, living standards would continue to
remain low and would probably fall for some groups. Direct
comparisons of wage and price levels were now significantly
absent.

BBC 1 21:00 16.2.79
(Prices without wages)

   If such comparisons *had* been broadcast, they would have
shown that wage increases at the time were, on average, barely
ahead of prices. Far from there being any 'wage explosion',
these settlements had no hope of recovering even the real
income levels of 1975. There were no headlines to announce
that fact, nor any which linked 'official' figures, showing the
fall in real income, to the industrial unrest of 1979. The
television news used official information to criticise the trade

unions for their alleged effects on the economy and on government policy. But the same figures were not used to draw conclusions which might be damaging to government policy, or which might question its economic logic or validity. Though the precise content of the news changed between 1975 and 1979, the organising principle remained the same. The news was still presented from the point of view of the government's pay policy: 'Good News' was measured in terms of how well this was doing. So instead of comparing wages with prices, the BBC on 14 February 1979 compared them with earnings in the preceding phase of the pay policy.

In a similar vein, ITN reported the new earnings figures as follows:

The authorities were happy to announce two bits of economic news today. First, Britain made a profit of a million pounds last month; they'd thought the balance of payments might be much worse because of the lorry drivers' strike — but it wasn't. And second, the official figure for earnings is that in the five months until the end of December — that's the first five months of Stage Four — they rose by just 3.4 per cent. That included the Ford settlement, but *the total of workers settling was only a million.*
                                                        (ITN 22:00 14.2.79)

Only a million? With such a small number, apparently, ITN could not find any of them to see if they were as 'happy' with the figures as the authorities were. Two days later ITN juxtaposed their report on retail price increases with a NUPE pay claim:

... the government will be able to say that the increases in basic rates which the unions are resigned to, have been kept to a strict nine per cent — and that amounts to a significant morale booster in the battle against inflation.

This assumes not only a direct link between wages and prices as the source of inflation, but also that the battle to be fought is against wages, rather than, for example, against unemployment. And for whom are these figures supposed to be a "morale booster"? Many economists believe that allowing wages to fall in real terms must produce high rates of unemployment. There is no single analysis which everyone accepts. *The Financial Times* noted (8.2.79) that while some experts suggested higher wages would produce real growth, others argued almost exactly the reverse.

It is only because the BBC and ITN argue consistently from *one* point of view that they are able to use concepts such as 'wage inflation' and its 'dangers' quite uncritically, and to express 'hopes' and 'fears' from within such partial and limited assumptions. What is 'reasonable' and what is 'excessive' is determined from within the same limits. An interview with the Prime Minister on BBC 1's *Nine O'Clock News* (8.3.79) was introduced with these words: "Mr. Callaghan has been concentrating a lot this week on the government's stand against excessive pay claims." It would be difficult to imagine such an uncritical reference to trade union policies — for instance that they had been 'concentrating a lot on getting a living wage for their members'.

On *News at Ten* the same day, Mr. Callaghan was reported in the headlines as saying: "There's no more money." In the interview itself, which was shown on both channels, he commented: "You can't get more money out of the bank than there is in it." The interview was reported in conjunction with the government's decision to restrict credit by putting up interest rates. An ITN reporter underlined the whole message by declaring that the decision "reinforces the government's determination to stand firm in the face of mounting pay claims. Mr. Callaghan won't print what he calls 'confetti money' to finance these claims."

At no point in this coverage were any of the government's economic assumptions challenged. In the interview, there are no interruptions; nor do we see any questions put to Mr. Callaghan on the news programmes of either channel. He gives his message unchallenged, direct to camera. Yet within the current political and economic spectrum, a wide range of critiques was available. On the same day as this interview, *The Financial Times* argued that the government's pay policy was a series of '*ad hoc* stop gaps', with each year's limit having no special coherence. Just three days earlier, on 5 February 1979, *The Financial Times* had attacked the very calculations which were being used to relate wage increases to inflation and unemployment.

While there is no sustained critique on the television news of the 'official' figures, or of the views of the 'authorities', there *are* severely critical analyses of calculations and claims made by other groups such as trade unions. Perhaps there is a fear — felt by the BBC and the IBA alike — of offending the powerful. 'A million workers' can be dismissed without worrying about the consequences, but the Cabinet, the Bank of England and the Treasury are altogether more immediate and potent forces. But such coverage leads inexorably to the view that working people are responsible for the crisis and that it is acceptable that they should pay for it. Alternative ways of understanding the crisis and other possible ways of resolving it are excluded. In the next chapter we look at how journalists intervene in political coverage to establish this view of the world.

IV
"PUSHED ABOUT BY THE LEFT"
Labour Politics on Television

*... he described a conversation he had had with Tony Benn, M.P.,
in the course of which Mr. Benn had re-stated his well-known
criticism of the BBC's coverage of politics, claiming it concentrated
on personalities rather than politics; that the BBC traditionally
inhabited the old centre ground of the man of good will and intent;
and that it portrayed this centre ground as being held by people like
Jim Prior, Ted Heath and Shirley Williams who were the good
guys and girls with whom most of those who worked for the BBC
sympathised on a personal level. In doing so, Tony Benn claimed
that the BBC was taking sides in a battle going on within the two
main parties themselves. (Our correspondent) said he had
countered these suggestions vigorously but he had wondered
whether there was not a grain of truth in some of them somewhere.
(BBC Confidential News and Current Affairs Minutes, 13.1.81)*

This is a study of how politics is treated on television news. It is
mainly concerned with coverage of the Labour Party. As such
it is at the heart of what broadcasters most pride themselves on
— the fair treatment and presentation of parliamentary
democracy. But our findings are disturbing: they show the
television news to be in violation of the broadcasting acts and
conventions themselves. The news is neither balanced nor
impartial nor even accurate in this key area.

> It should be the duty of the Authority to satisfy
> themselves that so far as possible the programmes
> broadcast by the Authority comply with the following
> requirements: That is to say . . . that due impartiality is
> preserved on the part of persons providing the
> programmes as respects matters of political or industrial
> controversy or relating to current public policy.
>
> *(IBA Act 1973)*
>
> The licence requires the BBC to refrain from
> editorialising.
>
> *(BBC Handbook 1977)*

For this study we have taken a number of samples. The first
comes from the period when the Labour Party was in power
and relates closely to our material on economic coverage. It
demonstrates how left-wing policies such as Labour's Industry
Bill fared on the news. The second sample comes from the
period after 1979 when Labour is in opposition. The political
debate here is not only over policies but also about the nature
of the Labour Party itself. This study involved a detailed
analysis of interview questions, statements made by journalists
and information and comments which they have chosen to
report. We recorded all television news programmes each night
for three weeks in the period following the Labour and
Conservative Party Conferences (20.10.80—10.11.80). The
main story in this period was the struggle for the Labour
leadership following the resignation of Jim Callaghan. In
addition, we analysed a number of other news and current
affairs programmes on later issues such as the deputy
leadership campaign, to see whether the tendencies and
patterns we had found were constant over a long period.

Realism and Socialism

The news treats political views and policies of the right quite
differently from those of the left. Healey's budget in 1975 was
presented as a necessary and realistic response to 'high' wage
awards. Healey's views and warnings were constantly "rubbed
in" by reference to 'official' information and authoritative
sources. Rationality and hard 'realism' are presented as the

prerogative of only one view — his. What is apparently the pragmatism of the 'actual' world is set against the 'political' demands of the left. This view is summarised in this BBC commentary on the budget: "One of our Westminster staff said criticisms and praise were evenly matched. Right-wingers said the budget was realistic, left-wingers said that it wasn't socialist." (BBC 21:00 16.4.75).

The possible rationality of left-wing policies is not explored in the same way. The core of the left case on inflation and economic decline was that these resulted from the decline in private investment, sometimes referred to (though not on the news) as 'a strike of capital'. There were a small number of references to the problem of investment, but these were greatly outweighed by references to wages and wage inflation. The reasons for the decline in investment (for example that capital was moved abroad) remained unexplored. In general the decline in investment, where it was mentioned, was treated rather as a natural and unavoidable disaster. The left's case, that investment is critical to an understanding of both inflation and economic decline, appeared only in brief and fragmented references. There were only three of these in the whole four month period of our study and all were reports on the views of Tony Benn. He was quoted as follows:

The Industry Secretary, Mr. Benn, today gave his explanation for the country's industrial failure, for which he said working people had become the most popular scapegoats. The real cause was lack of investment, and he said inflation was the result of overpriced goods produced with outdated equipment by underpaid workers.

(BBC 21:00 25.1.75)

One solution proposed by Tony Benn was the Industry Bill of 1975, which was intended to reverse the decline in private investment. Ten days before it was introduced in the Commons, the Department of Trade and Industry produced figures predicting a disastrous fall in industrial spending on plant and equipment. These crucial figures were reported on the television news in January, but significantly were never used to explain or justify the Industry Bill, which was reported quite separately. On the news, only some warnings are "rubbed in". Because the rationality and logic of the left case is absent, the news may present it as mere utopian dreaming.

In television coverage of the 1979 Labour Conference, the simple assumption that the right wing has a monopoly of 'realism' is again evident. On BBC 2, for example, a journalist commented: "Two conflicting themes have dominated this conference — the call of principle, the demands of reality." (BBC 2 23.00 3.10.79). This coverage starkly illustrates central features which recur over the following two years. The desire for change towards 'democracy' in the party is shown as the prerogative only of the left and is represented merely as an attempt at crude control. Through all this runs the media's obsession with Tony Benn.

At the conference a call was made for change in the party's organisation: essentially for a shift in power from the Parliamentary Labour Party to the National Conference and to constituency parties. Inside the Labour Party, there were three sets of opinions on the proposed changes. The right wing opposed them and attempted to dismiss the debates as foolish internal squabbling, fomented by the left to further their own ends. They demanded party unity, based broadly on the existing party structure and their position within it. The left case was that internal democracy (and party reform) was necessary to reflect grass-roots opinion and to establish an alternative socialist strategy — such a platform had to be worked out before seeking re-election. A third group supported the constitutional changes on their own merit, and did not identify themselves with the 'left wing'.

The BBC's coverage pursued the views of the first group — that it was all down to the machinations of the left. This was, of course, hotly disputed by many in the party. Thus a journalist interviewed Frank Allaun:

BBC JOURNALIST: Can you deny that the object of these reforms is to ensure greater left-wing control of the party, Mr. Allaun?

ALLAUN: I certainly do. I say the object of these reforms is to make the party more democratic, so that the parliamentary leaders respond to the decisions of the rank and file.

(BBC 2 13:00 1.10.79)

And a later interview with Eric Heffer:

JOURNALIST: How do you feel that the left has fared . . . ?

HEFFER: Well, I'm not sure you can actually say it's just the left who want reselection . . .   (BBC 2 23:00 2.10.79)

There is a notable absence of such questions as: "Mr. Healey, can you deny that your calls for unity are no more than an attempt to avoid criticism of the last government?" A central theme for the BBC was that the constitutional changes were intended to ensure greater left-wing control of the party. The proposals for democracy and accountability appeared merely as a facade behind which the left could work. One of the key proposals was that the National Executive should have ultimate control over the content of the party's manifesto. Of 17 references made by the BBC to the decision on this, 13 were introduced as either "another victory for the left wing" (BBC 1 19:30 31.10.79), "strongly supported by Mr. Benn" (BBC 1 17:40 31.10.79) or "a serious defeat for Mr. Callaghan" (BBC 1 12:45 31.10.79). Only two references described the changes as having anything to do with 'democracy' and 'accountability'.

Such coverage has the function of isolating the left and of downgrading their case. More seriously, it involves a major distortion of the range of views inside the Labour Party. The beliefs of those who favoured reform but who were not on the left were substantially ignored. This was commented on in *Labour Weekly* by R. Websdale, a delegate who had moved one of the motions for reform: "I am astonished that the commitment to democratise is viewed as the prerogative of solely the left wing." (5.10.79).

The amount of attention given to Tony Benn is extraordinary. A range of policies are presented as though they 'belonged' to one individual, rather than having any broad support within the party. On Wednesday 3rd October the BBC covered the conference's vote on the party's manifesto and a speech by Benn (ITN was on strike at the time).

NEWSCASTER: Mr. Benn's day at the Labour Party Conference
REPORTER: Very much Mr. Benn's conference, then ...
(BBC 1 12:45 3.10.79)

NEWSCASTER: An ovation for Tony Benn, as the Labour Party Conference at Brighton gives the National Executive control over the party's manifesto. The change, strongly supported by Mr. Benn, was carried ...
REPORTER: So Mr. Benn won the two most significant of the three votes he needed to change the balance of power within the party. (BBC 1 17:40 3.10.79)

NEWSCASTER: An ovation for Tony Benn ... The change on procedure, strongly supported by Mr. Benn ...

(BBC 2 19:30 3.10.79)

While BBC 1's, *Nine O'Clock News* bulletin referred only to Labour's "left wing", the visual display showed Tony Benn on the platform, and the conference delegates applauding. The "left wing" becomes synonymous with Benn. Even his absence is noteworthy. Interviewing Eric Heffer on BBC 2, a journalist persistently inquired why he, Heffer, rather than Benn was speaking for the Party's Executive:

JOURNALIST: Where is Tony, why is he not speaking in these debates? ... Are you not surprised to be replying to all these debates, not having Tony or anybody else?

HEFFER: I think the media really has gone out of its way to build up this picture that we're all creatures of Tony.

(23:00 2.10.79)

Benn is not given status in the same way as other political figures. On the following day, Healey appeared and was described on BBC 2's 7:30 News as "Shadow Chancellor" while on BBC 1's *Nine O'Clock News*, Benn was referred to simply as "Labour's leading left-winger". Our investigation of the leadership election pinpoints how Tony Benn is treated differently from other politicians and has a special role in the manner in which political life is represented.

The Leadership Election, 1980

We began by looking at the range of opinions that existed at that time in the Labour Party, primarily over the issue of internal democracy. There were other issues dividing the right and left which were raised briefly, such as campaigns over nuclear disarmament or membership of NATO. But these did not form the basis of major rows in the party at that time.

The second phase of our analysis was to examine which themes were taken up by television news and used to underpin and direct the coverage. The leadership struggle raised key issues, not just over who would win, but over how the leader should be elected. The right to select the leader was one part of the intensive debate which now raged over internal democracy. The 1980 conference had thrust to the fore all the different questions over how each section of the party was to relate to the others. Who was to decide policy? What were the relations to be between the National Executive and the Parliamentary Party, between MPs and their constituency parties, between these and the rest of Labour voters, and what was to be the role of unions in the party as a whole?

To the extent that television news covered these themes it did so almost exclusively from the point of view of the right wing of the Labour Party. We found here, that the news operated against not only left-wing policies, but the presence of the left in the party as such. They are presented as a persistent source of trouble and problems. What the left see as demands for democracy and for MPs to be accountable is presented on the news as merely a series of "threats" and "undue pressures". The effect of this was to produce a crude caricature of the left position and to miss out a whole range of other opinions at the centre of the party.

The immediate context for this construction was the 1980 conference and the attacks made by right-wingers such as Shirley Williams on alleged 'left fascism'. The vision of the left as an insurgent force, variously engaging in "bullying", "intimidation", "blackmail", "undue pressure" and "dictatorship", was a key organising principle for subsequent news coverage. Broadcasters did much more than merely report the views of the right. They effectively adopted these as their own, and channelled the flow of information to fit in with them.

Such coverage can in no sense be regarded as 'balanced'. On the same evening as Shirley Williams made her statements, other fringe meeting speakers were underlining what right-wing domination of the National Executive had meant in the past. One speaker recalled how his local party had been disciplined — their crime was that their banner had been taken on a CND march to Aldermaston. There were accounts of blacklists that had operated against left-wingers who wished to stand for election to Parliament. The news cameras were present at this meeting: such material could have been used; but autocracy is constructed in the media largely as a prerogative of the left.

In the whole period of this study there are 14 occasions when any person or group on the right was referred to as either "bullying" or as engaged in "illicit" or otherwise undemocratic behaviour. By comparison, there are 52 occasions when those on the left are reported as "bullying", "intimidating", "bordering on dictatorship" or in other ways acting undemocratically. There are also a small number of reports carried of the right and left denying these accusations.

The Labour Party is in its nature a highly diverse body, in which people and groups with widely differing ideologies are present. But the organising principle on which media coverage is based presumes that 'entryism' comes almost exclusively from the left. Little or no attention is paid to the activities of right-wing groups which do not accept the party's constitution — except when they are portrayed as the victims of "intimidation". There are no searches for 'blue moles'.

Once this general framework is established, then political questions are reducible simply to: is the left blackmailing and dictating or not? The coverage is then structured to answer this with a very firm, yes! What the left see as requests for information or consultation is constantly presented by TV journalists as forms of intimidation. Interview questions (on both channels) frequently repeat this theme. For example, one major story at this time was concerned with the letter sent by the Labour Co-ordinating Committee to local constituency parties. The letter recommended that MPs fill in their ballot papers for the Labour leadership at the General Management Committees of their local parties after a vote had been taken by party members. The people who sent the letter argued that members had the right to know how their MP was going to vote, and that he should know their views. They denied that this constituted an attempt to 'order' MPs how to vote. Michael Meacher, one of the letter's authors, pointed out that the word 'mandate' had deliberately not been used (BBC 2 *Newsnight* 20.10.80). Even if it had, it is not clear why to 'mandate' somebody should be regarded as undemocratic. Still in this case, the left argument was that they had not wished to go even this far, and that the letter insisted only that there be consultation and open voting. As Tony Banks summarised it in *The Guardian*, "representatives should not need secret ballots" (22.10.80). The right-wing opinion of the letter was that it did constitute an attempt to order MPs how to vote, and that this should be regarded as a form of blackmail. If MPs did not represent the views of their local parties, then they might not be reselected. Denis Healey termed this "a naked appeal to blackmail and fear".

The view of the right wing was overwhelmingly pursued by the television news on both channels. On only one occasion was the meaning of the letter interpreted by media personnel according to the view of the people who had sent it. On BBC 2 on the 20th it was reported as: "A letter recommending local constituency parties to summon their MPs to explain how they intend to vote." (*Newsnight* 20.10.80). The actual text of the letter was quoted three times. There were 10 occasions on both channels when it was interpreted by journalists according to the view of the *right*. For example on ITN it was referred to as: "... saying in effect that MPs should be made to vote as they are told" (ITN 22:00 20.10.80) and on the BBC as urging: "the constituency parties to order MPs how to vote in Labour's leadership election" (BBC 1 17:40 21.10.80). Whatever the 'real' meaning of the letter, the view of the right wing was that it should be regarded as blackmail and intimidation. This view is again overwhelmingly represented in the news in reported statements.

There are *three* occasions when the left was reported as defending the letter, as in this example from ITN: "The Labour Co-ordinating Committee have defended the letter saying it was only asking for honesty from MPs, not mandating, dragooning or instructing." (ITN 22:00 21.10.80). The right is reported *thirteen* times, referring to the letter in terms such as "bullying tactics" (BBC 1 21:00 20.10.80),

"naked blackmail by Mr. Benn's supporters" (ITN 17:45
21.10.80) and in headlines such as "Labour's right says left is
sending threatening letters" (ITN 22:00 20.10.80). On many
news programmes, only the right version is reported. When
references to the left case do appear, they have the status of
being mere tokens since the news is organised around the right
view in terms of headlines, correspondents' definitions,
interview questions and summaries. For example, in this BBC
programme the juxtaposition of the two views is preceded by
the journalist defining the letter in terms of MPs being 'told'
how to vote.

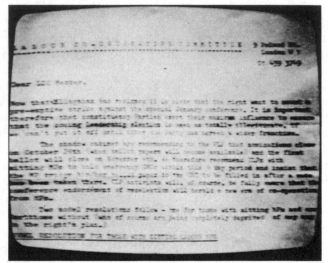

"Labour's right says left is sending threatening letters."

NEWSCASTER: Tonight, Michael Meacher MP and other
members of the left-wing committee on which Mr. Benn sits
have replied to a new attack about a letter they have sent to the
constituencies. It urges all local party members to tell their MPs
how to vote next month. The Committee's view: "We're asking
for honesty not secrecy." Mr. Healey's view: "It's a naked
attempt at blackmail."

(BBC 1 21:00 21.10.80)

It might be noted in passing that Mr. Benn does not sit on this
committee and has stated that he did not know the contents of
the letter until after it had been sent.

News programmes offer only an illusion of balance whereby

alternative views are presented as a kind of Aunt Sally to be knocked over in the dominant flow. The ITN news on the same evening has this headline: "Healey says left letter was blackmail." The report runs as follows:

NEWSCASTER: Mr. Denis Healey has launched a fierce attack on the left-wing Labour Co-ordinating Committee who are supporters of Mr. Tony Benn. In an interview with ITN he denounced a letter in which they urged constituency activists to tell their MPs how to vote in the leadership ballot as "a naked appeal to blackmail and fear".

This leads to an interview with Healey in which the journalist again pursues the same theme:

NEWSCASTER: This is what he told (our journalist) earlier today:

HEALEY: I found that absolutely disgraceful. It was a naked appeal to blackmail and fear . . .

JOURNALIST: But it is a real threat isn't it — that reselection — saying that you won't get your job back as an MP — it could swing the balance against you?

HEALEY: Well I don't think so. I think many people will be stiffened in their resolve by this naked attempt to blackmail them . . .

(ITN 22:00 21.10.80)

The interview with Healey is long, but at no point does the journalist take up the left theme that the whole argument is being used as a smokescreen by right-wing MPs who wish to avoid any form of consultation. After further questions on the new electoral system and why Denis Healey wished to be leader, the final question from the journalist on this news is: "Do you think Mr. Benn is out of touch with the average Labour voter?" After Mr. Healey's firm agreement on this, the newscaster returns and finally there is the brief reference to the left position:

NEWSCASTER: The Labour Co-ordinating Committee have defended their letter saying it was only asking for honesty from MPs, not mandating, dragooning or instructing. And Mr. Tony Benn has said he will only stand for the leadership after the new selection procedures are introduced. Mr. Benn told a Labour meeting in London "What's happening now isn't a real election. When there is a real election I will be a candidate".

In the summary at the close the dominant themes of this news are referred to again. Such summaries and headlines are important, because in them journalists compress what they take to be central in the news. While a number of accounts and comments may be present in the whole programme, only some survive for reiteration. The concluding summary for this news is:

> NEWSCASTER: Mr. Denis Healey has strongly attacked the left-wing Labour Co-ordinating Committee, who are urging local constituency workers to tell their MPs how to vote in the leadership battle. Tonight an ITN poll shows Mr. Healey just ahead of Mr. Foot.

(ITN 22:00 21.10.80)

That the news pursues the logic of one set of political beliefs is shown very clearly in the structuring of interviews. Journalists sometimes claim that they deliberately play the part of devil's advocate and ask 'oppositional' questions to whoever is being interviewed. This is supposed to provide lively television and vigorous probing of issues. But in the case of this story, it did not happen. The same assumptions were overwhelmingly pursued whether a right-winger was being interviewed or a left-winger such as Michael Meacher. He had appeared on the BBC 2 *Newsnight* programme the previous day. This item is introduced as follows:

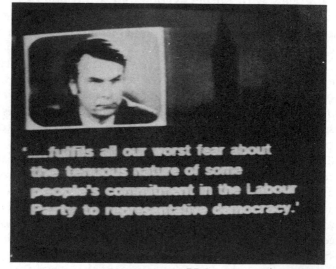

'...fulfils all our worst fear about the tenuous nature of some people's commitment in the Labour Party to representative democracy.'

BBC 2 Newsnight 20.10.80

NEWSCASTER: And Labour's far left gave another stir to the Party's troubled waters tonight. They were calling on constituency parties to insist on ordering their MPs to write in their choice of Labour Leader on his ballot paper. I will be talking in a moment to the left spokesman, Mr. Meacher, and to an MP on the right of the party, Mr. Mike Thomas.

(BBC 2 *Newsnight* 20.10.80)

The interview is introduced with a quote from the letter and a reported statement from David Owen:

INTERVIEWER: Dr. David Owen has tonight attacked the letter. The former cabinet minister and leader of the right-wing Campaign for Labour Victory called on all candidates to condemn it. It was not the time, he said, for weasel words. He said: "The letter fulfills all our worst fears about the tenuous nature of some people's commitment in the Labour Party to representative democracy."

Well now, Michael Meacher, can you tell us, some MPs might accept, quite a lot of them, that they are accountable to their constituency parties. Are you now saying that they must quite simply take orders from you?

MICHAEL MEACHER: We are not saying that at all. There is no question of a mandate, the word mandate isn't used and we are not recommending there should be a mandate on MPs.

All the questions put to Meacher follow the same assumptions. The two which follow are:

INTERVIEWER: But in the discussion here it says he must present his ballot paper to the GMC to be filled in after a vote has been taken. After the vote has been taken, must he fill it in with the name of the candidate being voted?

and later,

INTERVIEWER: When you say the CLP activists will of course be fully aware that the conference endorsement of reselection will herald a new era of co-operation — does that mean that you think that the constituency should somehow threaten the MP? If he doesn't vote the way they want him to, they should sack him?

When the interviewer turns to the right-wing MP, his question is: "Now Mr. Thomas, are you going to take your ballot paper to your constituency management committee and ask them how you should vote?"

Mike Thomas replies that he will not, and that when he casts

his vote it will be as a representative of 18,000 Labour voters in
his constituency. The only time that a 'left-wing' question is
asked here, is when after this, Michael Meacher intervenes and
takes on to himself the role of interviewer.

MEACHER: Can I ask Mike Thomas how he proposes to take
the view of 18,000 members in his constituency. I mean is that
not really a complete fiction and doesn't it really mean that the
right wing of the party wishes there to be no discussion really
with their constituency party or even if there is discussion to go
away secretly afterwards and do exactly what they think
themselves?

There follows a heated discussion between Meacher and
Thomas, with each accusing the other side of being
undemocratic. Into the fray steps the interviewer and once
more channels the discussion into a 'right' framework, in a
further question to Meacher:

INTERVIEWER: To take up on Mr. Thomas's earlier point,
you talk about a wider franchise. Why are you going back to
your constituency now to ask them how you should vote for the
leader — on talking to only 20 or 30 members of your local
Labour Party. Why not to the thousands of them ... "

MEACHER: I would very much hope we have a meeting when
thousands of people will come, but let me say this about the
GMC, so far from being — I don't know what it is in Newcastle
East, it isn't a smoke-filled room in Oldham — it is a
representative group ...

(BBC 2 *Newsnight* 20.10.80)

Such coverage establishes a very specific image of the left.
They come to be associated with 'trouble' as naturally as
Leyland comes to be associated with 'strikes'. The first
sentence of the above report establishes the theme: "And
Labour's far left gave another stir to the party's troubled
waters last night". The powers of darkness are assembling and
we are being warned. From the same bulletin we have: "Within
the lower reaches of the party tonight ... there is a darker
mood."

In this coverage the alleged influence of Tony Benn is a
pervasive theme. The politics of the Labour Co-ordinating
Committee are denoted by a series of references to him.

He was angry about a letter from the left-wing Labour Co-
ordinating Committee *in which Mr. Tony Benn is involved.*

(BBC 1 21:00 20.10.80)

The Labour Co-ordinating Committee, *a group close to Mr. Benn,* have sent a letter ...

(BBC 2 *Newsnight* 20.10.80)

A committee *closely associated with Mr. Tony Benn urges the constituency* parties to order MPs how to vote ...

(BBC 1 17:40 21.10.80)

Tonight Mr. Michael Meacher and other members of the left-wing committee *on which Mr. Benn sits** have replied to a new attack.

(BBC 1 21:00 21.10.80)

The letter sent by *Mr. Benn's friends* in the Labour Co-ordinating Committee ...

(ITN 17:45 21.10.80)

The left-wing Labour Co-ordinating Committee *who are supporters of Mr. Benn* ...

(ITN 22.00 21.10.80)

"And to ensure a balanced and impartial discussion of the latest government measures, I have with me a government spokesman and a wild-eyed Trot from the lunatic fringe."

* Tony Benn does not sit on this Committee.

These references are important in the context of a sustained anti-Benn and anti-left campaign. We showed how in industrial and economic coverage the pattern of how to understand 'strikes' and 'wage claims' is laid down very thoroughly in some parts of the news. Later the constant monitoring of these makes sense without having to be actually told all the time that wages = inflation. If a newscaster says, "and now another wage claim" we can be expected to know what is implied. The references to who is involved with Tony Benn operate in a similar fashion. Television takes its cue from the press and performs the major function of pointing out what Benn is involved in and who knows him. Of course there is nothing wrong in reporting what Benn or any other politician is doing, but in these cases the labels and the commentary are used as a substitute for debate. There is no real analysis of what is going on in the party or who is arguing for which policies. Instead we have simply the latest 'trouble' from the left and Benn. The story is not initiated as an account of the Labour Co-ordinating Committee or its intentions, but is rather the latest set of complaints about them.

The Language of Struggle

The television news acts as a compère when describing conflicts within the party, but is clearly standing on one side of the ring. If the left win then the language may be of trouble and turmoil. For example, the events of the 1980 party conference were described on BBC1 as: "The Labour Conference has been plunged into turmoil tonight over the dramatic result in the way Labour's leader is elected." (BBC1 21:00 1.10.80). But if the right hold off the "trouble", "turmoil" and "stirs" of the left, then the story may be told quite differently. In the period of our study, there are a number of arguments between Labour's National Executive Committee, which had a left-wing majority, and the Parliamentary Party, which was more to the right. In one such conflict, the left argued that the leadership election should be delayed until after the new electoral college was set up. The outcome of this struggle is referred to quite differently: The "moves" of the left wing are now being "thrown out".

Well, it's almost certain that the party's MPs will throw out the

NEC call for a delay.

(BBC 2 *Newsnight* 22.10.80)

It is almost certain that when Labour MPs meet next Tuesday,
they will throw out the NEC's proposal.

(BBC 1 14:00 22.10.80)

Labour MPs have thrown out moves by the left wing to
postpone the party's leadership election ...

(BBC 1 *Late News* 28.10.80)

The words 'move' and 'bid' are much more frequently used to
describe the actions of the left than of the right. In isolation
these words cannot be taken to prove anything. But their use
in the overall context of the coverage is part of a pattern in
which the left is presented as an insurgent force, against which
others "firmly assert" their rights:

NEWSCASTER: *A left-wing move* to make public the way MPs
vote was also defeated. Here is our political correspondent ...
JOURNALIST: By defeating *left-wing moves to* postpone the
election Labour MPs have *asserted firmly their right* to choose
their own leader whatever the rest of the party does.

(ITN 22:00 28.10.80)

The NEC is not referred to as "firmly asserting its rights". It
simply "wants to put off the leadership election"
(BBC 1 19.00 22.10.80). In such coverage, "left-wing moves",
"trouble" and "domination" go together quite effortlessly.
The following day, the National Executive is again reported as
arguing with the Parliamentary Party.

The *left-wing dominated National Executive* had rejected pleas
by ... Mr. Denis Healey and Mr. Michael Foot that Labour MPs
should be given more time to express their views on how the
party leader should be chosen in future.

(BBC 1 21:00 29.10.80)

The word "domination" takes on a very specific meaning in
such a context. It is not used to mean anything so simple as
having a 'majority'. In the whole of the period analysed, *only*
groups identified as left-wing are referred to as "dominating".
Thus we have the "left-wing dominated National Executive",
"the left-wing dominated constituency parties" (BBC 1
Nationwide 20.10.80) but "heckling from the right-wing
majority" (ITN 28.10.80).

One reason why the words "domination" and "left-wing" go together with such ease in this coverage is that the views of the right wing on "intimidation", *etc.*, are featured much more often and more prominently than the views of the left in headlines, summaries and especially interview questions. After the meeting on 29 October when the left on the NEC had "rejected" the "pleas" of Healey and Foot, there is a statement to camera by the right-winger David Owen. He argues on BBC 1 that the National Executive is "bouncing" the conference and is thus acting undemocratically:-

DAVID OWEN: . . . The Parliamentary Party have no view other than the decision they took before conference against an electoral college and the general feeling is that we are being bounced, into a situation in which the NEC comes forward with model resolutions much too soon without genuine consultation with the Parliamentary Party.

(BBC 1 21:00 29.10.80)

The view of the left is, as we have seen, that it is the Parliamentary Party who wish to avoid consultation. David Owen is not questioned on this by the interviewer, but rather his version is taken up and used as the basis for questioning others leaving the meeting.

INTERVIEWER: Some of the Shadow Cabinet think they are being bounced.

NEIL KINNOCK: I think one or two of them always say that. They seem to be extraordinarily bounceable. I don't think anybody was bounced on either side or in any respect whatsoever this morning, and it would be fiction for anybody to say that they were being bounced.

INTERVIEWER: (*to Michael Foot*) Some members of the shadow cabinet feel they have been bounced this morning.

MICHAEL FOOT: Well, I don't know. I don't answer such questions as that because you are putting words in their mouths and you are not putting any in mine.

INTERVIEWER: You don't feel bounced?

FOOT: No, I don't feel bounced . . .

(BBC 1 21:00 29.10.80)

The ITN main news that night concluded its section on the meeting with the statement from David Owen. It follows the latest odds on the leadership candidates and a brief interview with Michael Foot.

NEWSCASTER: . . . Mr. Healey did everything he could to look
the confident favourite today as he went to the joint NEC
Shadow Cabinet meeting. Mr. Peter Shore was unruffled
though the smart money says he could be the first to go, or if not
him, Mr. John Silkin, but Mr. Foot seemed happy.
FOOT: I am always optimistic. Nothing could ever make me
anything other than optimistic.
INTERVIEWER: One commentator put you this morning as
favourite.
NEWSCASTER: The Shadow Cabinet were unhappy. Dr.
Owen said he felt MPs were being bounced.
(ITN 22:00 29.10.80)

The statements by Michael Foot and Neil Kinnock, which
contradict this view, are not included here.

The following night ITN again highlights the theme of left
"intimidation". The trailer at the end of the first half of *News
at Ten* states: "Mr. Michael Foot, standing for the leadership
of the Labour Party, says MPs should not be intimidated by
their constituency parties. He talks to us in Part Two."
(ITN 22:00 30.10.80). What has happened is that both of the
main contenders to the leadership are being pressed by
journalists into commenting on the alleged 'activities' of the
left. In an interview shown on this ITN news, Michael Foot
replies by specifying the rights of each section of the party. His
exact words are as follows:

> Members of Parliament have got the right to exercise their
> judgements   that's what they are there for. They have got the
> right to exercise their judgements in their choice and selection
> of their leader and their deputy leader and their Parliamentary
> Committee and they know how to do that and I'm against any
> form of intimidation against them doing their job. Of course
> they can consult with their General Management Committees
> and most of them do, and their General Management
> Committees have got a right to say to them "We want you to
> consult us", but the Member of Parliament must exercise his
> own rights and I'm sure Labour members are going to do it.
> (ITN 30.10.80)

It is this reply that has been represented as him saying, "MPs
should not be intimidated by their constituency parties on
how they vote." The selection of his words tends in the
direction which the news is systematically pursuing. From the

same text he could just as easily have been reported as saying, "Michael Foot has reasserted the rights of constituency parties on consultation with MPs". But ITN has chosen to highlight criticisms of the left, just as on the previous day it concluded the NEC report with the comments of David Owen.

The chosen theme in discussing the constitutional issue is this "unreasonable pressure". The interview questions put to Michael Foot on this were as follows:

(1) INTERVIEWER: (Are you) a bridge builder, a peacemaker inside the party?

FOOT: Well, yes, but not a caretaker ...

(2) INTERVIEWER: Are you the sort of man who can be *pushed about by the left* inside the party if they pushed you into standing against your will?

FOOT: They didn't push me into standing against my will ...

"Are you the sort of man who can be pushed about by the left ... "

(3) INTERVIEWER: If you are a bridge builder in the party, is there not a real struggle going on to control Labour MPs, by the party outside, and can you avoid taking sides on this?

FOOT: Members of Parliament have got the right ...

(4) INTERVIEWER: More specifically they have an absolute right to vote for whom they like in this election.

FOOT: Of course they have that right ...

(5) INTERVIEWER: There was a recent letter that suggested that local parties might reselect or sack an MP who went against their wishes.
FOOT: No, I'm against such a proposition and this is a distraction.

(6) INTERVIEWER: (Is it) unreasonable pressure?
FOOT: Yes of course. This is a complete distraction ...
                                        (ITN 22:00 30.10.80)
Not all of these are in fact questions. The fourth one is a statement about the rights of MPs and the second simply assumes the behaviour about which questions are apparently being asked. The BBC also pursues the same theme in an interview a few days later. In all this, Michael Foot is in an invidious position, since the clear implication of some questions is that he is in receipt of 'dirty votes'. These supposedly come from illicit behaviour and "intimidation"— the existence of which the media has done so much to establish. As in the following exchange from the BBC interview:
INTERVIEWER: Many MPs have been asked very openly by their constituencies how they will vote in the election. A lot of that pressure has been in your favour. *Do you accept that a significant number of your votes may have come from this pressure, and if so are you happy with that act?*
FOOT: No, I'm against any form of intimidation ...
INTERVIEWER: What do you say to any MP who is under *this sort of pressure?* What should he say?
FOOT: An MP in my opinion should consult with his local party. ... but he's not there to be dictated to by his local party. He must use his own judgement ...
INTERVIEWER: He should use his own judgement even if he runs the risk of reselection and losing that afterwards?
                                        (BBC 2 *Newsnight* 4.11.80)
By such processes of highlighting, selection and endorsement, the news gives credibility to one account over others. There is an almost total absence on the news of the point of view that "this sort of pressure" might be quite reasonable or democratic. Whatever the Parliamentary Party thought, there

is no doubt that many people in the constituency parties believed that MPs should be subject to a democratic mandate. The senders of the LCC letter maintained that all they were asking for was an open discussion. But even if they had suggested a mandate it would not be acceptable for 'neutral' media to promote the view that this was "undue pressure" and "threats". One news programme did film, without comment, a local party meeting (*Newsnight* 30.10.80). It showed quite clearly the stark difference between the normal media view and that of many local members who argued simply that Labour MPs should represent the views of the party. It showed also an intense and rich debate on the nature of the party, its history, and what it was to become. It raised many questions and issues on the right and left which were absent from the rest of the news — Was Healey a monetarist? Could any of the candidates be trusted in the face of patronage and secrecy in Parliament? The range and depth of the arguments put into sharp relief the shallowness of the rest of the coverage. Nearly a half of this in our sample was taken up with predictions and questions on who was going to win and the latest odds from Joe Coral, rather than the issues that the election was about. This one programme was so startling because it violated a pattern in which when issues *are* discussed, journalists see them through the eyes of the right wing of the parliamentary party, and peer downwards with curiosity and some alarm at the "pressure" from below. The news is effectively being orchestrated around this view, which is tacitly and sometimes explicitly endorsed. There is a great difference between asking someone their opinion and simply *assuming* that people 'threaten' or 'push others about'.

It would be impossible for journalists to work without seeing the world through political perspectives, but what is disturbing is that at present they are constructing these overwhelmingly in one direction. What is at stake is the entire way in which the social and political world can be understood. The news is profoundly committed to a distinct social and political order. The preferential treatment accorded to some right-wing views is only a part of this. A second critical feature is the closing off of possible alternatives. Information which contradicts the preferred view or which would give credibility to the alternatives, is either rewritten, downgraded or simply left out. The attempts to democratise the Labour Party are presented as if they are themselves undemocratic. The 'pressure' from below is to be closed off and a favourite theme of media coverage becomes the question of how democratic is the Labour Party at its base? Who is pulling the strings?

In the press, this general theme is taken up by conservative writers in everything from headlines in *The Daily Express* through to the television column in *The Observer*. While *The Express* reports on "HOW A MARXIST PACK IS HUNTING DOWN ITS QUARRY" (9.6.81), *The Observer* comments that, in a television interview, Tony Benn was asked "every question except the awkward one about just how democratic the new democracy within the Labour Party really is" (7.5.81).

On television news, block votes, militants, and activists are all earnestly discussed. And of all the smoke-filled rooms that the news likes to investigate there is none more so than Barnsley where the "domination" is from "Scargill's miners" (BBC 1 18:05 1.11.80). A week after the letter controversy, the latest Barnsley story breaks on BBC 1. It combines all the favoured elements of "intimidation" and "dictatorship" by the left.

NEWSCASTER: Now an item of late news: Mr. Roy Mason, former Northern Ireland Secretary, in a speech tonight to his Barnsley Constituency Party, has spoken about what he called "threats and intimidation bordering on dictatorship" in the election for the labour leadership. Mr. Mason says he has considered the views of his Constituency Labour Party, but in the end he would use his own judgement over whom to vote for. His statement was made in reply to a party left-winger who wanted him to support Mr. Foot, or face not being reselected as Barnsley's Labour Candidate.

(BBC 1 21:00 31.10.80)

The late-night news headlines also pick up the story:

NEWSCASTER: Mr. Mason spoke tonight of "threats and intimidation bordering on dictatorship" from left-wingers in the Barnsley Constituency Party who supported Mr. Foot.

(BBC 1 31.10.80)

The coverage is structured in such a way that the left are normally on the defensive. They are reported less frequently, and as giving denials to the latest set of allegations which have been selected and presented by the news. On the following day the BBC reports that:

NEWSCASTER: Yorkshire miners' leader, Mr. Arthur Scargill, has denied trying to dictate how Labour MPs should vote in the election for the party leadership, but he said any MP who ignored the constituency committee ran the risk of not being re-selected.

The finger is now pointed at who is really dominating whom, as the newscaster goes on:

Mr. Scargill's miners dominate the Barnsley Constituency Party which has ordered the ex-Cabinet Minister, Roy Mason, to support Michael Foot. Mr. Mason has defied them as (our journalist) reports:

JOURNALIST: Last night the Barnsley Party Management Committee voted four to one to instruct their MP to vote for Mr. Foot, but Mr. Mason told the meeting that the miners shouldn't bludgeon MPs into submission and talked of "threats and intimidation bordering on dictatorship". Some delegates said that Mr. Mason, a former miner, might lose his NUM sponsorship, but as he left the meeting, no one was any the wiser where he would be putting his cross on the ballot paper.

There follow brief interviews with Mason and the Constituency Chairman.

MASON: Well I mean, it looked to me that they were instructing me to vote for one man, and demanded to see my ballot paper. I didn't think that was right and proper. I explained that I wasn't a delegate and I shall use my judgement. Although I lost the vote, by the way.

INTERVIEWER: Who will you be voting for?

MASON: Well that's not for you to know, that's for me to decide. I haven't decided yet.

INTERVIEWER: But did you tell the Committee tonight?

MASON: No.

INTERVIEWER: (*to Party Chairman*) Did Mr. Mason give you any indication at all which way he is prepared to vote?

CONSTITUENCY CHAIRMAN: No he didn't, and quite honestly as Chairman of the General Management Committee of the Barnsley Constituency Labour Party, I'm very, very disappointed at that. As the General Management Committee we have the right to know, on this particular issue, bearing in mind the amended constitution.

(BBC 1 18:05 1.11.80)

The allegation is that the left are intimidating and domineering — in all this it is quite clear where the BBC stands. Scargill, the miners and domination just seem to go together. The theme is repeated in the next news: "Last night, the Barnsley Committee, dominated by miners, ordered him to confirm in advance a vote for Mr. Foot ... " (BBC 1 20:50 1.11.80).

But do the miners dominate in the way that is suggested here? The Barnsley constituency is large and the Management Committee is a very big meeting. It includes delegates from eleven constituency branches (who send six each) and from other members' branches in unions such as ASTMS, AUEW, NUPE, TGWU, USDAW, ASLEF, GMWU, NGA, SOGAT, COHSE, NACOD as well as the NUM. It also has a number of delegates from the women's section, the Young Socialists and the Co-operative Movement. According to the official minutes, there were 123 delegates at the meeting that night. The vote that Mr. Mason refers to as having lost was so overwhelming that even if *none* of the miners delegates had voted it would still have been carried by a ratio of more than two to one in favour of Foot. The truth is that the miners' delegates are not in a majority, they could not determine such votes even if they wished to, and in fact they do not have to, given the weight of the rest of the opinion in the local party. This opinion is, of course, totally absent from the news, which is organised around the alleged domination by miners. There is no account given of the other groups represented at the meeting or of the actual voting figures. The only reference to these is on the above BBC news, when we are told that the committee has voted "four to one to instruct their MP" (BBC 1 18:05 1.11.80).

It is not clear from this description that there were any more than five people at the meeting. It is not explained that this is a ratio, that the meeting was extremely large, or that there were delegates from numerous branches. In all the other news programmes, even this reference is dropped. This story could just as easily have focused on an overwhelming vote for Michael Foot from a constituency party, but the chosen theme was 'domination' and of Mr. Mason being "ordered" and "told to vote for Mr. Foot" (BBC 1 20:50 1.11.80). This version was embraced by the BBC, but was hotly disputed by the local

party secretary who made the following statement:
> I wouldn't say it was an order. There was no order placed on Mr.
> Mason whatever. Considering the party was in favour of Foot,
> we fully expected Mr. Mason to support that view, but there
> was no order in any shape or form. If the media wishes to give
> the opinion that Mason was ordered it simply isn't true.

No such statement was given on the television news. The only
appearance from the local party was the constituency chairman
being asked whether Mason had revealed his vote. This
interview was then dropped from the subsequent news,
though the one with Mason was retained.

Much of the television news which we analysed for this
study directly paralleled coverage in the conservative press.
This was so in the general direction of stories and in the
assumptions which informed them. Television would simply
offer a less hysterical confirmation of what people read in the
papers. Thus the Barnsley constituency was the subject of a
major exposé in the London evening paper, *The New
Standard*. The story was headed "HOW THEY PULLED THE
PROPS FROM UNDER MASON". According to the sub-head,
the paper was about to reveal: ". . . the astonishing story of
how Arthur Scargill has won control of the Barnsley Labour
Party.Is this the pointer to where and how Labour goes from
Wembley, as the Left tightens the grip?" The thrust of this
story is "ruthless exploitation" by the left and Arthur Scargill
in particular. We are told that:
> In Barnsley, as on all its battle fields, the left has exploited
> ruthlessly the reluctance of rank-and-file party members to take
> part in public showdowns . . . Many moderates have simply
> stopped coming to party meetings. They find it difficult to
> summon heart . . .

(The New Standard, 22.1.81)

This comment does not appear to have been borne out by the
large number of delegates who attended the party meeting
with Mason, but our central point is how television gives
credence to such themes. While the conservative press is
mounting something of a hue and cry about Arthur Scargill,
the BBC quietly affirms that "Mr. Scargill's miners dominate
the Barnsley Constituency party". It thus legitimises one set
of views and probably does so with a greater authority because
of its quieter manner and its supposed impartiality. Because

the groundwork is laid so thoroughly, it does not need to overstate the case. When, for example, the industrial editor of ITN uses a phrase such as "the likes of Arthur Scargill" (ITN *Lunchtime News* 6.9.80) in discussing a pay claim, we can be expected to know what he means.

The language of pay claims and 'trouble' in industry is in fact very close to that used in describing political life. The left-wing in politics are cast very firmly into the role occupied elsewhere by Leyland car workers. We showed in our analysis of Leyland coverage that workers are said to "reject" while management makes "pleas":

> They *rejected* a *plea* to call off the strike which could cut production by a thousand cars a day.
>
> (ITN 3.1.75)

The same formula occurs in describing the thorny relations between the NEC and the Parliamentary Party, where the latter is very firmly in the role of management. We heard above that: "The left-wing dominated National Executive had *rejected pleas* by ... Mr. Denis Healey and Mr. Foot ... " (BBC 1 21:00 29.10.80).

The Deputy Leadership

Six months later this formula is still being used when Tony
Benn decided to stand for deputy leader. Mr. Foot is still
reported as making "pleas" and "appeals" and being
"rejected":

> Mr. Tony Benn has *rejected* an *appeal* from the Labour Leader,
> Mr. Foot, not to stand against Mr. Denis Healey in the deputy
> leadership elections this Autumn. Mr. Benn announced his
> candidature during last night's all-night sitting after *rejecting
> two pleas* by Mr. Foot. Today Mr. Foot repeated his *appeal* . . .
> So it's not surprising that, among his constituents in Bristol
> tonight, he showed no sign of *yielding to Mr. Foot's plea.*
>
> (ITN 2.4.81)

And on the BBC:

> Labour Leader Mr. Michael Foot has publicly *appealed* to Mr.
> Tony Benn to reconsider his decision to contest the deputy
> leadership. Mr. Foot had *appealed* to Mr. Benn privately not to
> do so . . .
>
> (BBC 1 17:40 2.4.81)

> *Numerous appeals* to him to change his mind have so far failed.
> In his constituency tonight, Mr. Benn made it clear to (our
> reporter) that he was *rejecting* Mr. Foot's *appeal.*
>
> (BBC 1 21:00 2.4.81)

> Labour leader Michael Foot publicly *appeals* to Tony Benn not
> to contest the party's deputy leadership.
> Mr. Foot had appealed to Mr. Benn . . .
>
> (BBC 2 19:35 2.4.81)

> Tonight in Bristol he rejected Mr. Foot's appeal.
>
> (BBC 2 *Newsnight* 2.4.81)

The analysis of such language is difficult, since the use of
individual words such as "reject" and "plea" or "dominate",
changes over time. It might be possible to find individual
examples of their use which are different if people look hard
and long enough outside the periods we have analysed. But it
does seem clear on the basis of our very extensive sample that
there are major differences in presentation. Workers are not
reported as "pleading for a living wage". Benn is not reported

as making a "plea" for an open election on policy issues and being "rejected".

The use of such language is one part of the presentation of Benn as an isolated maverick. Political coverage is as usual presented from the 'top', in this case the Parliamentary Labour Party, which effectively excludes most of Benn's support. ITN at one point acknowledge that Benn's strength is not in the PLP, but is in the conference and in the party's grass roots in local constituencies and trade unions. (ITN 17:45 2.4.81) Yet in all of the news coverage of Benn's decision to stand for the deputy leadership on BBC 1 and ITN, we never hear from any of this support. The only person who appears on these programmes in favour of Benn standing is himself. He is interviewed in all three of ITN's news programmes on the day. In the lunchtime news and in *News at Ten* the interview is 'balanced' with John Silkin declaring his opposition to Benn standing. The commentary in ITN's news is largely a catalogue of those who are opposed, "exasperated" and "appalled":

A new leadership row has broken out in the Labour Party over Mr. Tony Benn's decision to stand for election as Mr. Foot's deputy.

Mr. Foot says he does not want an election for his deputy to be held this year. He says it will detract from the job of fighting the Conservatives.

Mr. Benn is challenging Mr. Healey, who was elected to the job before it was decided to give a bigger say in leadership elections to the unions and local parties.

Now Mr. Benn promises a six-month campaign before the election at the party conference in October — a campaign his critics say will divide the party when it should be united in fighting the government.

Labour MPs should not have been surprised by Mr. Benn's decision: but the great majority of them think that he's profoundly mistaken — and *very many are appalled*, including some who like him but who'd hoped to persuade him not to take a step which, they fear, will keep the party divided for the next six months, and delight the Conservatives and the breakaway Social Democrats.

Mr. Benn's strength has never been at Westminster, among MPs, but in the party conference. *But never have Labour MPs*

shown such exasperation with him as today. They point out that
Mr. Healey was elected deputy leader unanimously only last
November. If Mr. Benn cared at all for party unity (was one
typical view expressed today) he would not be doing this.
   He's even divided his natural allies in the left-wing Tribune
Group. Some of them are sponsoring him. But others, even
while he was declaring his candidature early this morning, were
calling in vain for a meeting to try and stop him.

(ITN 17:45 2.4.81)

The news commentary on BBC 1 is also largely taken up with
reporting who is against Tony Benn, although it also carries
brief references to the policies on which Benn is standing, and
analyses the timing of the decision. But the news begins with
the opposition:

NEWSCASTER: Good evening:
There's a new leadership row in the Labour Party and Tony
Benn is again at the centre of it. He intends to challenge Denis
Healey for the deputy leadership later this year — and *numerous
appeals to him to change his mind have so far failed.* Mr. Benn
believes his move will help party unity . . . but his critics, from
the left as well as the right, totally disagree. *Many are angry*
about the prospect of another leadership battle, and say his
timing couldn't have been worse. Labour leader Michael Foot
this evening asked Mr. Benn to reconsider.
MR. FOOT: I believe it would be in the best interests of the
party if there were no contested leadership elections this year.
NEWSCASTER: He also urged Mr. Benn to take account of the
advice he was receiving, in and out of Parliament. But in his
constituency tonight Mr. Benn made it clear to our reporter he
was rejecting Mr. Foot's appeal.

(BBC 1 21:00 2.4.81)

Nationwide on BBC 1 interviews Reg Race in favour of Benn
and 'balances' it with John Silkin against. But on this day, only
Newsnight on BBC 2 shows people from the 'constituency
rank and file' speaking in support of Benn. It has also then a
long interview with Ian Mikardo, MP, in favour and Judith
Hart, MP, against.
   In subsequent weeks, the campaign for deputy leader was
the focus of a great deal of news and current affairs. It was in a
sense the perfect opportunity to look at the views of people
outside Parliament as well as the political establishment. But

television journalism experiences great difficulty in doing this. Programmes such as *Nationwide* offer an illusion of representing 'the people' by simply stopping some in the street and giving them a few seconds each.

When television does attempt to look at grass-roots movements it remains trapped in the crude stereotypes utilised by those who peer from the top of society down at the strange activities below. A politician such as Benn has to lose out in such coverage, since in 'politics from Parliament' he appears as an isolated maverick, while support for his views at the base is compressed into the tight categories of "far left", "hard left", "militant", "activists", *etc.* When such terms are used in a pejorative sense, they operate largely to pre empt debate — they are not much more than name calling by the media. Their use simply obscures who actually believes what, and the nature of support for different policies.

It is apparent from our conversations with news journalists that many of them really believe that the views of what they call the "far left" are held only by a small minority. Even though analyses of public opinion show a wide section of people who support opposition to the Common Market, and who are against nuclear weapons and the stationing of cruise

missiles, *etc.* Of course such evidence on public opinion does not mean that the mass of the population is consistently radical — the same people may hold 'left' views in some areas and be 'right-wing' on others such as capital punishment. But television does very little to clarify such differences, since issues and policies are displaced by the running commentary on the latest incursions by the "dominating", "hard", "far left". It is the range of opinions and the different groups who hold them that is missing. This applies not only to Benn and his support, but operates against alternative politics in general, since television presents the world from a viewpoint that is somewhere between the Social Democrats and the right wing of the Labour Party. Some journalists are aware of this but the limits within which they work mean that they are constrained to the 'normal' channels of description, the 'acceptable' and 'official' sources, and the reliable, high-status 'experts'.

Coverage in depth?

This pattern extends both to news and current affairs. We looked in detail at a BBC *Panorama* programme on the deputy leadership campaigns. It is important, not because it is in any sense 'worse' than other programmes at that time, but because it raises in a single report a very large number of the themes which were at stake. It was entitled *Vote, Vote, Vote for Tony Benn* and the structure of its main report was as follows:

1. Introduction: a report on "tactics of backroom boys who are urging Labour to Vote, Vote Vote for Tony Benn".
2. Clip of Benn speech on "policies more important than the person".
3. Benn coming out of hospital.
4. Report on Benn's supporters — shots of meeting of rank and file mobilising committee.
5. Two clips of speeches by Benn and one by Healey.
6. Report on history of Benn's move to left, and quote of Foot saying "Tony, you are going nuts". Report on changes in party constitution.
7. Clip of Benn speech defending his decision to stand as deputy leader.
8. Sidney Weighell interview attacking Benn's decision.
9. Reports on (a) secret meetings between D. Healey and right-wing leaders and (b) the history of Benn's decision to stand for deputy leader.
10. Interview with Joe Ashton, MP, criticising the timing of the decision.
11. Report on Benn's support in constituencies over shots of him at garden fête plus brief comments on the extent of his

travel schedule.
12. Introduction to ASTMS conference as being like American primaries.
13. Benn at ASTMS conference plus Clive Jenkins against and one other speaker in support of Benn.
14. Denis Healey with Frank Chapple at electricians' conference plus demonstration by "dissident" electricians.
15. Speech by Healey denouncing Trotskyites.
16. Shots of meeting of 'Militant Tendency' with three speakers.
17. Report of Foot's challenge to Benn to stand for leader.
18. Interview with Joe Ashton defending last government and attacking Benn.
19. Shots of meeting in support of John Silkin, beginning with image of him as a rubber dummy in Union Jack waistcoat.
20. Healey speech on solidarity movement.
21. Interview with Benn on coach.
22. Interview with Sidney Weighell attacking Benn.
23. Shots of train and quote of Benn on Chinese Philosophy.
24. Interview with Michael Foot.

In this example the central themes for coverage are again taken up very explicitly from the right-wing press and are explored in a way which is marginally more genteel by the BBC. On 20 June, 1981, Mr. John Silkin, a rival contender for the deputy leadership, made some remarks on what he called Tony Benn's "American-style" electioneering. These were elaborated on the following day by the *News of the World*, under the headline "FURY OVER 'VOTE BUYER' BENN". The story began: "Tony Benn received a blunt challenge last night to declare how much of his private wealth he is ploughing into his campaign for the Labour Deputy Leadership." (*News of the World* 21.6.81). The *Panorama* programme was on the following night and in it the "American-style" of Benn's campaign is simply assumed. It is highlighted in an advert for the programme. In the actual event, we are told: "This weekend, John Silkin and his supporters demanded that Tony Benn reveal how much he's spending on his American-style election campaign." (*Panorama* 22.6.81).

As evidence for the American nature of this campaign the programme had already provided a rather unlikely comparison of British trade union conferences with the primaries of

American elections:

> In Benn's campaign, the big trade union conferences became like
> the American primaries: USDAW, ASTMS, and the T & G,
> equalled New Hampshire, Alabama and California.

Even if this comparison is accepted, it is not clear what Tony
Benn is supposed to be doing that makes his campaign
'American' as distinct from that of Denis Healey. Both are
shown addressing a number of trade union meetings. Tony
Benn apparently does more of these, and according to the
programme has support from "a range of radical left-wing
groups" — but we were left wondering which American
election *Panorama* had in mind with radical left groups at its
centre.

For such allegations to appear on the BBC, as opposed to the
News of the World, there is a need for 'hard evidence',
particularly on finance. It is apparently provided at the
beginning of the programme with an analysis of Tony Benn's
supporters. While the *News of the World* makes assertions on
"Benn's fortune" and has headlines on 'Vote Buying', the BBC
quietly confirms that:

> Only Tony Benn has a paid election organiser, Jon Lansman. He
> is the secretary of the umbrella organisation of eight left-wing
> groups — the rank and file mobilising committee.
>
> (Panorama 22.7.81)

After the programme, the committee referred to stated that
Tony Benn had given none of his personal income to the
campaign. More significantly, Jon Lansman, who was
supposed to be the "paid campaign organiser", complained to
the BBC that he did not receive a salary as the committee's
secretary. He made a statement of the total amount received
by him for subsistence and expenses in the period referred to.
It came to just £323.

Much of the rest of this *Panorama* report was taken up with
analysing the campaign and views of Healey and Benn, with a
brief section on John Silkin. Benn's views are taken up first and
are summarised by the reporter: "His message was
unmistakably clear: that Labour's leaders in Parliament have in
the past and will in the future betray the wishes of the rank and
file unless they are made directly accountable."

Benn's voice is then heard making these accusations, while
we are shown clips of past Labour leaders. At this stage, the

programme is quite clearly critical of Healey. The reporter notes of his speeches that: "With his own policies so far out of favour, he confines himself to generalities and the odd joke." Later, he is reported as meeting "secretly" with "right-wing leaders of trade unions whose votes were vital to him". The message is clear — that Healey is an old-style leader who is out of touch with the rank and file. By comparison Benn is shown as having more support at this level. An ASTMS meeting attended by him is referred to by the reporter as "the biggest fringe meeting in the union's history".

Healey's critique of Benn is also explored. The allegations reported are that Benn is a "little Stalin" and Healey is shown attacking Benn and the left as "relying on help from communists and Trotskyites". These allegations are backed up in the programme by cutting from Healey's speech to shots of pamphlets on Trotsky and Lenin, and finally to a meeting of the 'militant' group.

The BBC commentary underpins Healey's comments:

DENIS HEALEY: ... they rely on help from Communists and Troskyites who reject parliamentary democracy in principle and they use bare-faced lies to support their campaign of vilification.

REPORTER: (*over shots of Trotsky and Lenin*) One of the groups most fervently supporting Tony Benn is the Trotskyist Youth Movement, the Militant Tendency.

"One of the groups most fervently supporting Mr. Benn . . ."

The programme is critical of both sides, but this does not mean that it conforms to criteria of accuracy or balance. Instead of a detailed analysis of the composition and support of both groups, we are offered a set of inaccurate caricatures. The only very clear thing revealed is that the programme makers don't like either group very much.

In the case of Denis Healey, while it is true that he is an 'old style' politician, and the revelation of the 'secret meetings' might be seen as good investigative journalism, this is clearly not the whole story of why he has support. If the opinion polls are to be believed, he must have some in the rank and file of the unions and in constituency parties (as was shown to be the case in *Newsnight* 30.10.80). In the whole programme this is never raised and no supporter from the base of the party is asked his opinion. There are in fact no specific interviews with anyone from the rank and file. Even though the programme is largely about campaigns and mass meetings it is still stuck in the familiar television mould of politics from the top. The commentators are either a journalist, professional politicians or trade union leaders. Only the last two of these are granted the status of being interviewed, and only the journalist looks straight at us out of the screen to explain how our world works. Other people are shown speaking or arguing but they mainly function as a sort of wallpaper over which the BBC commentary is fitted. Much of this latter is on the nature of Tony Benn's support. For example, the comments on Jon Lansman are spoken over the top of a pro-Benn campaign meeting. The message in the commentary is very clear:

> Benn is supported by a range of radical left-wing groups whose power has grown up outside Westminster. Their publications depict Tony as the man to end the routine betrayal by Labour's Parliamentary leaders of the rank and file. Only Tony Benn has a paid campaign organiser, Jon Lansman. He's the secretary of the umbrella organisation of eight left-wing groups: the rank and file mobilising committee. Last week its supporters responded to an appeal for money for the deputy leadership campaign. The different groups provide a ready-made campaign machine for Tony Benn and they have considerable experience of *mobilising party activists* in the constituencies and the trades unions.

(Panorama 22.6.81)

Here, the word "activist" is used to mean those who are mobilised by the Tony Benn "campaign machine". In such shots, voices come and go talking about "leaflets" and "meetings", but the main message is superimposed. This is so in the next reference to "activists", later in the programme. We are shown a different meeting, and hear a disembodied voice saying, "It's been a hectic month, comrades." The voice fades and over the top comes the reporter's message: "The Campaign for Labour Party Democracy has lobbied for ten years to make Labour's leaders and MPs directly accountable to *local party activists.*"

In the sense in which the programme is using the word "activist", this statement is quite false. The proposals for democratising the Labour Party drew support from a range of people, across the party. It has been a source of great irritation to people in the centre of the Labour Party that the new proposals were presented as if they related only to the left wing. As we showed above, it occasioned correspondence in the Labour press at the time of the 1979 Party Conference. It is quite clear that the proposals lobbied for by the CLPD gave everyone a vote, not just left "activists" and consequently drew a wide band of support.

This reveals a central flaw in the programme which is fairly typical in media coverage of the Labour Party. A large number of groups and individuals with different policies, tactics and beliefs are bundled up into what is called by the BBC "a range of radical left wing groups". The groups are given token appearances, but it is the commentary on their behaviour and 'tactics' which defines how they are to be understood. In the *Panorama* programme only the 'militant' group is actually shown at a meeting making a series of political points. But to use this group as representative of the left in the party is not accurate. A high proportion of their members come from the Young Socialists. A very brief sojourn at Labour meetings would reveal to BBC journalists that there are many on the left who regard the militants as at best idealist and doctrinaire and at worse as a source of painful ammunition for the right.

We do not wish to argue that the militants are irrelevant or should not be covered — but rather that the Labour Party is by its nature a diverse body with a very wide set of currents and opinions within it. These should be presented as they are.

There is a danger in television reporting that all critical voices be subsumed under the title of "hard left", while the commentators point their finger at the unacceptable politics. What people are actually saying is lost when catch-all phrases take in everyone from the CLPD to MPs who support Tony Benn, to trade unionists who dislike Frank Chapple.

Immediately before the Militant meeting sequence, *Panorama* shows a demonstration at the electricians' conference. The commentary runs:

> The left-wing of Frank Chapple's union accuse him of using strong-arm tactics to keep the union committed to the right. Coachloads of dissident electricians arrive to protest at the Healey-Chapple alliance ... as Healey entered the conference hall, the *hard left* staged a demo.

"Coachloads of dissident electricians ... "

There are shots of placards and of a "dissident" going to the rostrum without permission. The sound is faded and the commentary intones: "Both Denis Healey and Frank Chapple well understand the tactics of the far left as they've been communists in their youth." The reference operates as a dig at Healey and Chapple for their past, while the trade unionists are left with their present activity being described as "communist tactics". Neither group has the chance to answer. The demonstrators are protesting about their branches being closed, by Chapple. A close look at the placards being carried, using stop-frame video, shows one to be saying, "THERE ARE NO COMMUNISTS ON THIS PROTEST". But they are labelled by the BBC just the same. The demonstrators are simply wallpaper for a commentary which then leads directly to Healey's attack on 'Troskyites' and finally to the 'Militant' meeting.

As we have said, the programme makers clearly do not think very much of either side. Occasionally, this hostility breaks the surface, most obviously in relation to Benn and his supporters. They are said to "*endlessly claim* that his campaign is not about personalities". Benn is referred to as "the *darling* of the constituency parties" and as "the most *assiduous attender* of constituency party functions". More significantly, the treatment of Benn is unique in that of all the political figures discussed only criticism of him is delivered straight to the camera by a journalist. In a section on the history of Benn's campaign and the groups behind it, we are told of a series of informal meetings held by the left-wing ministers in the last Labour Government. The reporter tells us that they met over dinner, and in recounting the story he sits at a desk and occupies a position normally used by a newscaster, presenter, or some form of expert. He looks directly at us, and the camera closes on his face to accentuate the punchline.

Benn arrived after dinner apparently to say goodbye. He astonished his fellow-diners by telling them that he thought that Britain was turning into a police state; that as a minister his own 'phone had been tapped and that the country was ruled by the Civil Service. According to one of those present, Michael Foot summed up their reaction when he said:
(camera close up)
Tony, you're going nuts.

Later, there are two other references to criticisms made by Michael Foot. One comes in the middle of the showing of a speech by Tony Benn. The sound is faded for the reporter to comment: "Michael Foot accuses Benn of preaching the politics of the kindergarten. And though he never mentions his name, Foot is Tony Benn's unmistakeable target." The third reference quotes Foot's well known challenge to Benn to stand against him for the position of leader. In the second part of this *Panorama,* Michael Foot is interviewed by David

Dimbleby, and disputes the words attributed to him. He says
at the beginning:

> I think the film we've seen — by the way, I don't agree with all
> the details of it, some of the words that were put into my mouth
> I wouldn't accept . . .

Michael Foot is not denying that he has ever been critical of
Tony Benn, so it is presumably the context of his words and
the effect they are used to produce that is the problem.
Television constantly selects and organises information in
order to tell particular kinds of stories. It violates criteria of
accuracy by 'fitting' the world into its preferred views and is
also unbalanced in that it pursues some of these views over
others. In this programme, there are nearly twice as many
criticisms of Benn and the left reported by the journalist as
there are about Healey and the right. Benn and his supporters
are on the screen more, but a good part of this is interspersed
with commentary or is simply 'wallpaper' in the way that we
have described.

More significantly, while the programme includes criticisms
of both sides, only the right and those against Benn are invited
to reply in interviews. The two people interviewed for this
purpose are Joe Ashton, MP, and Sidney Weighell of the
National Union of Railwaymen. Four separate clips of them

speaking were interspersed in the programme such that they answer criticisms as they are raised and act as a running critical commentary on Benn. Joe Ashton is shown defending the last Labour government and criticising the timing of Benn's decision to stand as deputy leader. The last interview is with

"Tony . . .   . . . you're going nuts."

Sidney Weighell, where the left case is put to him for his reply:
REPORTER: Mr. Benn says that the top priority is policies not personalities and to ensure that the 'next' Labour government, when it gets to power, abides by the policies of the Labour Party Conference.
SIDNEY WEIGHELL: And what's he going to be, the new Messiah is it? Where is the evidence that people, the other leaders, or other people are going to renege on policies? The last government carried out something like 90% of the manifesto during its term of office. That's absolute clap trap and he knows it . . .
By contrast, no one on the left is asked to reply to the criticisms and commentary made on the programme. When Benn is interviewed by the reporter the questions put to him are:
You have got a punishing schedule because you make an enormous amount of speeches?

Do you think its been a good year for the Labour Party, so far
this year?

Do you think that the turn of the tide means that you'll be
elected deputy leader of the Labour Party?
The makers of the programme told us that they intended to
interview Benn again, but were prevented by his illness. But
this merely acknowledges that a large gap exists in the
programme. If a 'moderate' or 'reasonable' Benn supporter
had been allowed to speak, then many of its central themes
might have collapsed.

Reselection

On television the same range of stereotypes about the left in
politics is employed whether the issue is the leadership
election, the campaign for deputy or reselection. On the last
issue, the television news again parallels the right-wing press.
The over-riding theme is the incursions of the unacceptable
left as seen by the acceptable right. We saw how a potential reselection in Bradford was described in *The Daily Express* as
"HOW A MARXIST PACK IS HUNTING DOWN ITS QUARRY"
(9.6.81). In Scotland *The Sunday Standard* described the
"constituency infiltration by extremists" under the headline
"LEFT 'SECRETLY POISED' TO OUST MP'S" (*Sunday
Standard* 26.4.81). The actual reselection of Mr. Eric Ogden,
MP, in Liverpool was described in *The Glasgow Herald* as
"Mr. Eric Ogden is the latest victim of the far left's
exploitation of Labour's reselection process". (*Glasgow
Herald* 8.6.81)
    There are many more similar commentaries in the press, but
our main concern is to show how television acts to reinforce
these views on the latest "threats" from the left. In its anxiety
to pursue such themes the television news violates basic
criteria of accuracy and even logic. This was quite clearly the
case in the reporting of a motion on reselection passed by
Labour's National Executive Committee in May 1981. This
motion suggested that if in local parties there was more than
one nomination for the future MP, then these nominations
should be discussed. In other words, the sitting MP should not
be put on to a "short list of one" by the management

committee. The NEC was concerned that discussion in local parties was being pre empted, by a small group in the management committee simply pushing through the existing MP. But television resists the temptation to present this as a victory for debate and democracy. Instead it suggests that whole constituencies are happy with their MP, and only "Tony Benn and others" on the left-wing NEC are intent on forcing reselection upon them. Whatever the rights and wrongs of the case, it is logically absurd in a situation where a number of candidates have been put forward by different groups, to suggest that the "whole" constituency is happy with only one candidate (the existing MP). But undaunted the BBC reports:

"Mr. Benn and others have been unhappy that *some local parties who've no quarrel with their MPs* have simply put their name on a short list of one." (BBC 1 21:15 27.5.81). And later: "After the meeting it was announced that the National Executive will advise local constituency parties to consider other nominations, *even where they are satisfied with their sitting MP.*"

ITN follows the same pattern, reporting that: "*Local parties who are pleased with the way their local MP performs* have been getting round the rules in the view of Mr. Benn and his friends by nominating only a single person." (ITN 22:00 27.5.81). ITN is in fact even cruder than the BBC as it relates the whole complex debate in the NEC and the local constituencies simply to the alleged career intentions of Tony Benn. These are reported alongside a series of disparaging remarks on "Mr. Benn and his friends" and what they "call accountability":

Reselection of sitting Labour MPs is the single most important lever by which Mr. Tony Benn's influence in the Party is being turned into effective power. It was designed by the Left in the name of *what Mr. Benn and his friends call accountability* to compel every MP to face a challenge, so that if he habitually obeys the Party whips at Westminster so as to keep a Labour Government in business instead of obeying the wishes of the Party Conference then he can be slung out. It also means that he can be slung out if he fails to vote for Mr. Benn as deputy leader. And many Labour MPs who at first supported the idea of reselection, because they thought it was democratic, are now terrified of it.   (ITN 17:45 27.5.81)

Labour MPs are now "terrified" as the left hoardes
approach. The BBC is clearly standing on the same side of the
fence, as its journalists comment on the latest "threat" and
"pressure":
> ... the decision could mean some Labour MPs coming under
> *increased threat* from the left wing.
>   (BBC 2 19:25 27.5.81)
Some Labour MPs are worried that what has happened
today could make them *vulnerable to left-wing pressure* ...
(BBC 1 21:00 27.5.81)
No one is asked why the NEC has bothered to pass its
motion. The commentary and questions are from the point of
view of the beleaguered MPs. Eric Heffer is interviewed and
introduced with the immortal tongue-twister: "Did *left-
winger Eric Heffer* think that more MPs would now be in
difficulty?" There is also a brief interview with Betty
Boothroyd, MP, who is not denoted as "right wing", and is
simply asked, "how she felt about today's victory for Mr.
Benn". (BBC 1 21:15 27.5.81).
In all this the obsession with Benn continues even though
his own support is complex and there are many on the left and
indeed on the NEC such as Eric Heffer who do not
particularly support him at all. The focus on Benn goes beyond
merely the desire to inform on his actual activity or role.
"Tony Benn" and the word "Bennery" are important,
particularly in the right-wing press, as a symbol of all that is
supposedly unacceptable in the left. In these contexts, "Benn"
becomes another word alongside "far left" "hard left" or
"activist" as a way of pre-empting a real discussion of what
issues are at stake or who supports them for what reasons.

In other chapters we showed how the blame for industrial
and economic problems is most likely to be laid at the door of
the workforce. This diagnosis is then linked to a set of
preferred policies which are closest to the predominant views
in the Treasury, the right wing of the Labour Party and now
the Social Democrats. Working people have 'caused' the crisis
and now must pay for it via lower wages, 'acceptable' cuts, *etc.*
The significance of the political coverage which we have
analysed is that it closes off possibilities other than this, both
in the preference which it gives to some policies and in the

manner in which it describes the rise of the alternatives. Contemporary coverage of the Labour Party points very clearly in one political direction. The right is tainted with 'block votes' and 'secret deals' and on the left are the mindless militants. The hidden heroes are offstage, but the groundwork for the Social Democrats and their version of what is wrong with the Labour Party, is laid as firmly as if they had written the words. With the alternatives closed off, the way is open to the massive exposure which was given to the 'new' party.

"I suppose there isn't very much in the paper about the Indian railway crash because there weren't any Social Democrats on board."
(*The Guardian* 9.6.81)

It is not our intention here to mount a defence of the left wing or to suggest that such people are incapable of acting in a way which is undemocratic or intolerant. Given the mass and variety of people and groups involved in such a movement, it would be an unlikely proposition. Journalists are as free as anyone else to comment on mistakes or bad practice, or on the profound divisions which doubtless exist in the Labour Party. But press coverage which compresses a varied and profoundly felt movement into "Marxist packs" is clearly far beyond this. On television, the bundling together of left-wing unionists, militants, the LCC, constituency activists, friends of Tony Benn, plus anyone who supports democracy in the party, clearly results from more than simply political ignorance. There are many people in Britain who feel strongly about the new political issues that have been raised by opposition to the Common Market, by the campaign against nuclear missiles, the arguments over democracy and the demands for radical economic strategies in the face of depression. Such movements cannot be explained by reference to a few agitators or militants anymore than the riots in our cities can be explained by suggesting they are the work of "outsiders". Such 'explanations' serve only to pre-empt real discussion or analysis. It is the attempt to discredit the new politics that leads to the focus on the alleged activities of the "hard left". Real political alternatives in such a context must be presented as the products of a small unacceptable minority.

V
ACCESS TO TELEVISION

Access to the news is given mainly to the powerful. The view of social and political life that informs news production limits who is able to appear to put his or her case. It is a view of the world from the top downwards, in which those at the top do most of the talking. Restriction of access to a small minority of powerful people cannot be explained, in terms of 'shortage of time', mistakes by individual journalists, or difficulties of putting together a live news programme. These arguments may apply to an individual bulletin — but our evidence underlines that restriction of access occurs regularly over hundreds of hours of news bulletins. Over such a long period, arguments such as the shortage of time simply will not hold. They cannot explain the consistently one-sided nature of access.

"It's a Lot of Rubbish"

The case of the Glasgow dustcart strike pinpoints how television's view of the industrial world affects who is allowed to appear on the news, as well as the kinds of questions asked and the legitimacy and status given to different views.

The news established that the story of the Glasgow dustcart drivers was about the piling up of uncollected rubbish, the eventual official declaration of a health hazard, and the calling in of troops to break the strike and clear the rotting refuse. But the most remarkable feature of this coverage was that the workers who had apparently caused all this never appeared on the screen to explain their actions. The coverage began with reports of the decision of the dustcart drivers to go on strike. Yet the dominant television theme was never the dispute between the drivers and their employers (Glasgow Corporation), but rather its effects. From the very first day the frame was set that would exclude the strikers themselves and their

BBC 2 22:15 23.3.75

case. That day (Saturday, January 11) the BBC early evening bulletin carried a film report from Glasgow showing men leaving a meeting, over which it was stated that the decision to strike had been taken. We were then shown *library film* of piles of uncollected rubbish from a strike the previous year as the report continued: "It was only last October when rubbish piled up in the city streets for four weeks since Glasgow's dustmen staged their last strike for higher wages." (BBC 1 17:45 11.1.75). Other BBC bulletins that day showed similar cuts of old footage without including the new film of the break-up of the strike meeting. In each case the newscaster's message was equally sombre: "The decision to stop work from Monday was bringing fears of a repeat of the situation last October when rubbish piled up in the streets causing a health hazard." (BBC 2 22:30 11.1.75). This editorial speculation and forecasting was not restricted to the BBC. ITN also used old film on January 11 of the previous autumn's rubbish. The following day it reported: "The strike

means that Glasgow faces another pile-up of rubbish on the
pavements as happened for four weeks last autumn."
(ITN 22:00 12.1.75). Overall, a total of six national bulletins
that day used library film to highlight the 'effects' of a dispute
that had not yet begun.
The use of old film in this manner raises some important
questions. Is news a depiction of reality at a point in time or is
it an attempt to persuade the viewer that the events selected
have definite implications? In a sense these aspects cannot be
separated. News is never 'the facts' pure and simple, it
necessarily involves a selection, an analysis and, crucially, an
evaluation of reality. This is the work journalists do when they
'present the news' to their audience. Yet critics such as John
Birt and Peter Jay have suggested that a "bias against
understanding" exists in television news partly because of the
lack of background information in normal bulletin presentation. In answer to this the newsroom editors may have
congratulated themselves on the speed with which they
contextualised the Glasgow strike story by linking it to its
previous history. In this instance it is clear that the television
news did provide background information and understanding.
However, such information was selected from within a partial
viewpoint. The manner of the linking serves to provide a very
clear understanding — one might say a 'biased understanding'
— of the story, as being predominantly about another health
hazard. The fact that the old film carried a superimposed
caption stating the date of the events which it portrayed
entirely misses the point. We are not arguing that the
journalists attempted to mislead viewers into believing that
the rubbish actually existed then, in January. The point is that
such presentation could only lead to the conclusion that the
main issue of the current dispute was nothing more than a
danger to health caused by workers.
    It was not until seven weeks later that Glasgow Corporation
announced that a health hazard existed. By this time there were
real rubbish piles to film. Shots of black plastic bags lining the
streets and piled on open dumps became the familiar visual
image which symbolised the running story. What began as a
dispute between the dustcart drivers and their employers
became quite simply, "The Glasgow rubbish strike"
(BBC1 17:45 14.3.75), "The Glasgow rubbish" (BBC1 17:15

15.3.75), and headlined on News at Ten as "And now rubbish"
(ITN 22:00 21.3.75).

ITN 22:00 17.3.75

Reporting the Facts

If the news was so concerned to provide a context and
background to the dispute, why could more pertinent facts not
be given? We have shown that the kinds of information and
explanation that appear in the news essentially flow from the
dominant view. Alternative facts and explanations, where they
emerge at all, appear in fragmentary and sometimes
contradictory form. This is no less true in the reporting of this
dispute. What then was this strike really about?

The Glasgow Corporation drivers went on strike in the
autumn of 1974 in pursuit of pay parity with other Heavy
Goods Vehicle drivers. They were claiming an extra payment
to bring them in line with the minimum wage earned by drivers
in other industries. After four weeks the issue was still
unsettled but the drivers returned to work. This was on the
understanding that if national negotiations failed, then a local
agreement would be discussed. These facts are straightforward
and were available to anyone interested. The present authors
when speaking to the strikers during the 1975 dispute were
readily shown a photocopy of a letter from the Corporation to

the drivers' representatives giving just such a promise of local negotiations. This matter was covered on the regional news programmes on March 11. In *Scotland Today* and *Reporting Scotland* a spokesman read a statement giving the reasons for the strike action:

'The committee are still firmly of the opinion that they have a genuine grievance. They believe that the Corporation clearly promised to discuss the issue of a suitable payment at local level if national negotiations failed to provide an acceptable solution. The basic wage of HGV drivers with Glasgow Corporation is £32.50, the earnings referred to in last night's programme included bonus and at least 10 hours overtime payment. And there are Corporation drivers who only receive minimal bonuses. The lowest rate for a HGV driver in road haulage is £37.00. The committee are conscious of the effect of the strike on the public and would hope that the discussions they are now engaged in can provide the possibility of rapidly clearing the mountains of refuse now lying around the city.

(*Reporting Scotland* 11.3.75)

The closest the national television news came to the reason for the strike was on one bulletin on BBC. Speaking over film of parked dustcarts in a shed, it was reported that: "The men say their basic pay is £2.30 less than road haulage drivers and accuse the Corporation of going back on a promise to negotiate a local agreement." (BBC 1 21:00 13.1.75). This is not specialised or privileged knowledge — the journalists had the facts. Yet information of this kind was not generally given and was never used to organise or give coherence to reports.

Both channels emphasised that this was the second dispute in three months, without saying why this should be so. The effect was to give a picture of workers producing random chaos. This was mentioned in 13 of the first 14 bulletin reports following the strike decision and was still being mentioned in ITN reports about a fortnight later. Information concerning the earlier dispute was processed in terms of the dominant view. It merely strengthened the suggestion that the 'health hazard' was on the cards again. *News at Ten* on the second day of coverage repeated the showing of last October's rubbish; *Nine O'Clock News* was still showing library film on the third day.

The chosen angle governed the flow of news information.

Whilst reporting 'health hazards' and rubbish where they did
not yet exist, the current dispute that was supposed to have
caused them was not itself always mentioned. The dispute and
its causes almost disappeared from view. After several weeks of
the strike the City Authorities declared that a health hazard
existed and troops were brought in on the 16th March. That
day their expected arrival was reported on the BBC lunchtime
bulletin but the strike itself did not warrant a mention. The
BBC lunchtime news the following day reported the arrival of
the troops yet made no mention of the dispute except by
reference to "the dustmen who aren't involved in the strike".
Similarly, on March 20 ITN *News at Ten* and BBC early
evening bulletins both chose to focus on the difficult and
unpleasant task facing the troops without mentioning the
strike. From this point on, the progress of the army in clearing
the rubbish became a major preoccupation of news coverage.
Much use was made of film of heavy machinery, protective
clothing, the good humour of the troops facing picket lines and
chasing rats with sticks. Such exciting visual material was good
news for television. Soldiers even held up rats by their tails for
the cameras. These events fitted easily into the health hazard
angle.

BBC 2 22:15 23.3.75

When the dispute was included in reports however, it was with information that was confused and contradictory. The causes and the men involved were very much in the background. Who exactly was on strike and how many were involved varied bewilderingly. For example, on March 4 the BBC reported rubbish accumulated during "the strike by dustmen" (not dustcart drivers). ITN suffered similarly revealing confusion: "In Glasgow where the dustmen's strike, or rather the strike by dustcart drivers ..." (ITN 13:00 10.3.75). Meanwhile the news had reported the fact, and showed film to prove it, that the men who picked up the bins were not in dispute and were working alongside the soldiers. The account of who was on strike and the numbers involved varied from bulletin to bulletin. Thus the news spoke of "350 dustcart drivers", "550 men", "550 dustmen" and "500 dustcart drivers".

Other aspects of the dispute such as the facts of the men's claim were similarly affected by this coverage, either not appearing at all or being misreported. Of a total of 40 bulletins on the BBC only 4 mentioned a parity claim. An additional 7 bulletins referred to an "interim offer" or an explanation of the dispute such as "over pay". Of 19 reports on BBC 2 only 2 mentioned a parity claim. Three others reported the issue as "over pay" and one as over a "regrading structure". Of a total of 43 ITN bulletins, only 8 carried reports of a parity issue and a further 11 described the cause of the dispute as "over pay", etc. The narrow and restricted framework provided by the dominant view that produces such 'bad news' thus often leads quite simply to bad reporting.

A Hierarchy of Access

By news journalism's own standards perhaps the most glaring omission was that during the whole of the dispute not one of the strikers was interviewed on the national television news. In all, 10 people were interviewed, some of them appearing several times. The three news services together produced 20 national bulletins which included interviews with the following:

    a Professor of Community Medicine (4 appearances)
    a Fire Brigade Officer (one appearance)
    the Lord Provost of Glasgow (2 appearances)

the Secretary of State for Scotland (4 appearances)
a Glasgow Labour MP (one appearance)
a Labour Councillor (one appearance)
a Lieutenant Colonel (2 appearances)
a Second Lieutenant (one appearance)
2 TGWU Officials, Alex Kitson (4 appearances) and
George McGredie (one appearance)

BBC 2 22:15 23.3.75

This selection of interviews indicates whose views were deemed to be important. These are the legitimate and authoritative voices in terms of the dominant view. Once inserted into the logic and flow of coverage they constitute what amounts to an 'official view'.

The chosen definition of the news story provides the structure for the routine coverage and determines who will appear. It also frames the questions that are seen as important: 'Is there a health hazard?', 'How serious is it?', 'When is the Corporation going to act?', 'When are the troops being sent in?', 'How are they coping with the unpleasant task?' Given these priorities there is a hierarchy of access which logically excludes unofficial strikers.

As this was an unofficial dispute the interviews with the two union officials in no way represent a balanced coverage of 'both sides' of the issue. Only on the day the strike ended in defeat

were the drivers allowed to comment on their lost cause. ITN
reported that the 350 men were back at work "after their
abortive 13 week strike" and at last interviewed one of the
drivers. The report claimed that the drivers would "happily go
through it all again".
  TOM DOCHERTY: I would go on strike for the same cause
  again because we're qualified drivers ... We're experienced and
  we're professionals ... we are entitled to this money ...
  REPORTER: But going on strike doesn't appear to have
  achieved anything because the army can come in and do your
  work?
  DOCHERTY: Certainly, because we didn't have union backing
  this time.
  REPORTER: So why go on strike again?
  DOCHERTY: We'll go on strike on principle and we're still
  entitled to this money. And there's nobody saying we won't go
  on strike, we definitely will, if it comes to the cause again, and
  it's a justful cause, we must go on strike for it again.
                                          (ITN 22:00 14.4.75)
The television news, however, did not seem to think it was a
cause worth reporting.
  This is not an isolated or unrepresentative instance. The
routine restriction of access is further evidenced in our study of
economic coverage which we discussed above. Throughout the
period ITN's *News at Ten* and BBC's *Nine O'Clock News* kept
the range of views and opinions within a very narrow section of
the social and political spectrum. In news items dealing with
the social contract and its relationship to wages, prices and the
economy there were twenty-three different people interviewed, these were:
  The Prime Minister
  Three Government Ministers
  The President and the General Secretary of the CBI
  The heads of two nationalised industries
  Two MPs
  The General Secretary of the TUC
  Eleven leaders from national trade unions.
Among all these people there was only one 'ordinary' member
of the public: a senior consultant surgeon at Leyton Hospital,
Crewe. By contrast no miner, railway worker, power engineer,
electrician, doctor, postal worker, shop assistant or nurse were

offered the opportunity to give their views about the workings of the social contract.

"... AND NOW, A DISCUSSION ON WORKERS' CONTROL ...."

Apart from being interviewed or filmed whilst addressing a meeting, there are other ways of being featured on television news. Without appearing in person, one may be quoted directly, from a speech or from answers to journalists' questions. Such 'reported statements' are less powerful or prestigious than an appearance on the screen but nevertheless indicate that serious attention is being given. An analysis of these also shows a restricted access to news. Such statements come mainly from a narrow group. In this period, 35% of all reported statements on both BBC and ITN came from those interviewed in other bulletins. Within this select group the Chancellor of the Exchequer provided approximately 40% of the statements.

Taking all reported statements, including those from people not interviewed elsewhere, the Chancellor's share was still 14% on the BBC and 13% on ITN. Reported statements in general were mainly taken from members of the same narrow grouping:

12 from 5 Government Ministers
11 from 6 named Labour MPs
13 from other Labour parliamentary groups and sources
18 from 8 named Conservative MPs

7 from other political (parliamentary) parties and groups
6 from 5 other named Trade Union leaders
16 from other official Trade Union bodies and executives
21 from Government Bodies and Nationalised Industry managements
5 from employers groups, and 6 from the CBI
3 statements from the AA, a firm of stockbrokers and "financial observers"
3 statements attributed to "left-wing miners", "moderate miners" and "shopkeepers".

Shortage of Time?

It is often argued by journalists that they do not have the time and space to include all the views and information that surround a news story. While there are finite limits on what can be included, the selection process is consistently one-sided. What is involved here is not something that can be explained by errors, lapses of judgement or shortage of time. The Glasgow dispute was featured widely and prominently over a long period. It involved the professional judgement of several reporters and numerous editors in the newsrooms of all three channels. Rather the coverage consistently focuses on one view, while routinely downgrading or excluding others.

Television news does not merely restrict access, it also organises the flow of coverage around its preferred views. We have shown how statements from Healey as Chancellor, calling for wage restraint were accompanied by information and explanation that render such a view 'coherent' and 'reasonable'. Other alternative viewpoints are often excluded, but even when they are aired on television news they appear as disembodied fragments. The effect of such coverage is to accord status to some views as 'rational' and 'legitimate', while others appear as 'irrational', 'disruptive' and 'against the national interest'.

Access to Political Debate

In the coverage of the 1979 Labour Conference (limited to the BBC since ITN was on strike), the group that was selected to speak on the news was very narrow in its composition. There

were 100 occasions when people were interviewed or were
shown speaking. Of these, 86 were either the Leader of the
Opposition, Members of Parliament, or trade union leaders. In
a conference which was explicitly questioning the relation
between these groups and the Party's grass roots, the news
endorsed the view that it is the hierarchy who has a special right
to be heard. All through this period and later in the leadership
election, a major debate was being conducted in the party
branches and in the unions, concerning their future role in the
party. The main issues were: Should the leadership and MPs be
accountable to party members? What was to be the
relationship between conference decisions and the policy of the
Parliamentary Labour Party and any future Labour
Government; and should the election of the party leader be the
exclusive right of MPs?

The Parliamentary Labour Party was itself divided on such
issues, and it is reasonable to expect the media to seek out the
opinions of MPs involved in this debate. It is quite clear,
however, even by the media's own account, that the debate
taking place outside parliament in the constituencies was
central to the leadership issue. Thus a journalist on BBC 2
noted:

> For many in the Labour movement, next week's election,
> confined as it is to the Parliamentary Party, is just a stop-gap
> measure to pick a leader until new arrangements can be
> introduced to extend the vote to an electoral college
> representing the whole party. So already, therefore, there is an
> intense debate going on in the constituencies, not just about
> who should be selected but who should do the selecting and
> what sort of party he should lead.
>
> (BBC 2 *Newsnight* 30.10.80)

Clearly there is a wide diversity of opinions in the constituency
parties on the issues that *Newsnight* points to. The coverage of
the leadership issue took place against a back-cloth of
allegations concerning "left-wing dominated constituencies".
But rank and file members of the Labour Party were rarely
allowed to emerge from 'smoke filled rooms' into the clear
light of the television studio — certainly not in the case of ITN
and BBC 1. The familiar cast of interviewees included Healey,
Foot, Silkin, Shore, Owen, and Shirley Williams. We have
already shown that even with this limited range of

interviewees, questions put to them featured the alleged 'threats' and 'intimidation' said to be occurring in the constituency parties. Yet in the two main news services only

BBC 2 *Newsnight* 30.10.80

one individual is interviewed as a member of a constituency party. Enter stage left — the Barnsley Constituency Party Chairman. Having established that the Barnsley Party attempted to order their MP to vote for Foot, the only question put to the chairman was: "Did Mr. Mason give you any indication at all which way he is prepared to vote?" This pattern of neglect was paralleled in BBC 1's and ITN's selection of reported statements. A debate which is about the relationship between the grass roots of the party and MPs is thus channelled almost exclusively through the opinions of the latter.

Those interviewed and the number of appearances on BBC 1 and ITN news in our sample were as follows:

	BBC 1	ITN
M. Foot, MP	5	12
P. Shore, MP	3	3
J. Silkin, MP	3	4
D. Healey, MP	8	6

J. Lestor (NEC)	1	—
S. Williams (NEC)	1	—
D. Owen, MP	1	1
N. Kinnock, MP	1	—
R. Mason, MP	1	—
Barnsley Constituency Party Chairman	1	—
T. Benn, MP	—	1
Unidentified Speaker	—	1

This hierarchy of access was routinely followed on BBC 2 with two notable exceptions. In the aftermath of Foot's election, the reactions of constituency members on the left and right of the party were sought out. On October 30, *Newsnight* went to the constituency meeting in Islington and filmed, without comment, a discussion on the leadership. It showed an intense debate on the nature of the party, and questions were raised from right and left which were absent from the rest of the news. Ordinary party members felt quite able to indicate for example that they had never heard of John Silkin and could not see why he was standing. What struck us most about this particular coverage was simply that it was so rude and so honest. People on both sides said things about the candidates, about politicians in general and about our history which 'official' spokesmen and 'trained' journalists would simply not choose to say. The normal pattern of access is a product of the narrow understanding of social and political life around which television news is organised. It is quite 'natural' in this context for the news to exclude the voices of the powerless in our society.

VI

MASS MEDIA IN A CLASS SOCIETY

In Britain, almost everything we understand as mass communications, such as newspapers, books, records and films, is owned by twelve companies. They include household names like EMI and Rank and huge combines like British Electric Traction. Ninety-five per pent of the circulation of national daily newspapers is controlled by just five companies. The first and most obvious pressure on what the media produce comes from this pattern of ownership and financial control. Historically, this concentration of ownership gave immense power to a handful of people who used the media for propaganda purposes. The press is the most striking example. In 1948, Beaverbrook, the owner of *The Daily Express,* quite bluntly told the Royal Commission on the Press: "My purpose originally was to set up a propaganda paper and I have never deviated from that purpose all through the years." Other press barons promoted their political views by the same means, though not always to such extremes as Lord Rothermere. In the thirties he used his papers, including *The Daily Mail,* to give support to the Nazis in Germany and Oswald Moseley's Blackshirts in Britain. His headlines proclaimed "HURRAH FOR THE BLACKSHIRTS" and readers were given instructions on how to join the British Union of Fascists.

The influence of the individual press barons waned as their personal empires gave way to complex family and corporate organisations. But papers such as *The Daily Mail* have not lost the power to orchestrate public opinion. Popular themes of the moment are campaigns against nationalised industries, attacks on so-called 'scroungers' and the explanation of recent street riots in terms of the activities of 'outsiders'. These themes are obviously not chosen at the whim of individual proprietors; their origins are more complex. It is more accurate to see the journalists and editors and the mass media generally as one part of a society which takes private ownership, social hierarchies and profit for granted as the natural way of organising economic production and social relationships. The mass media have a critical role in the battle of ideas over how this society is to be explained and how it is to be justified. It is equally 'natural' then for the media to assume a role which defends and seeks to justify these social arrangements.

'... and at Question Time, MPs heard a hard-hitting attack on nationalised industry which brought loud cheers from Government back-benchers and the Press Gallery...'

Our economic system is built on a profound division between those who own and control capital and those who do not. This division between capital and labour has been more significant than any other in shaping our society over the last two hundred years. Each side of it has distinct and contradictory interests — what is profit and cash flow for the first is potentially wages for the second. From the point of view of those who own capital the main priority in initiating production is to gain the largest possible return for the money which they invest. But this endless search for profitability creates a constant tension with the labour that they employ. Industrial conflict is endemic to a system in which workers are permanently subject to the pressures of restrictive control, depressed wages and the threat of redundancy. The priorities of capital have meant that it will intensively develop some areas of the globe and then simply move on to where the pastures are greener — where labour is cheaper or where the conditions of production are thought to be better. In Britain, manufacturing industry has been starved of investment because it has been possible recently to make more money in other areas, such as speculation in land or food. This has encouraged stagnation, inflation and unemployment. One other effect of these 'normal' workings of the economic system is the frequent attempt to control wages.

The defence of these relations of private interest has rested on the assertion that the normal workings of the market economy will somehow benefit everyone within it. This is the ideology of 'consensus'. The problem with such a view is that the normal logic of the system does not promote equilibrium but produces crises and conflict on a large scale. Of course, when this occurs it has to be explained. The first rule of such an explanation in the conservative media is that there can be no fundamental antagonism between the two sides of industry. If there is evidence of 'trouble', it must therefore come from 'unacceptable' elements. There is a reluctance to scrutinise the actions of the middle or upper classes as a source of 'trouble' and even more of a reluctance to examine the economic system on which this class structure rests. The search for the source of trouble focuses instead on the actions of the workforce. Stories then abound of pig-headedness, wreckers, reds under the bed, exorbitant wage claims, strikes, people who are workshy, or think the country owes them a living. There is no comparable list relating to the activities of management or the owners of capital — there are no routine references to management intransigence, incompetence, expense account lunches, perks, fraud, manipulation of wage deals, lock-outs or tax avoidance. Most importantly, the economic mechanisms which regularly produce basic conflicts and decline are not routinely discussed as an explanation of problems such as unemployment and inflation.

There is a clear example of this in the coverage of the 'troubles' of British Leyland. The distribution of profit as dividends did not merit a headline, even though 95 per cent of the profits between 1968 and 1972 were distributed in this way.

The cause of lost production and of economic decline has to be the workforce. There can be no headlines saying:
A MILLION JOBS THREATENED BY HUGE DIVIDEND PAY-OUT.
And there is no routine referencing of the movement of capital away from productive industry. The consequences of such a movement and price increases are again laid at the door of working people. Figures on inflation are prefixed by figures on wage claims, but the amounts that insurance companies, pension funds and merchant banks have moved away from productive industry are practically ignored (in 1980, pension funds alone moved over £1,000 million into the buying of property). Recession, inflation and unemployment, if they are not being blamed on wage claims, were in the period of our study most likely to be treated as natural disasters. The world economy is presented as a kind of omnipresent force, and movements in it (balance of payments, exchange rates, cheap imports, *etc.*) are the problem, but these movements are rarely explained for what they actually are — simply people making money in the best way they can. A multi-national firm may be reported as regrettably being forced to close a factory in the North of England because it is uneconomic, but will not usually be spoken of as having made a *decision* to move its capital somewhere else because it can make more money there.

In the place of real explanations the leaders of business and government appeal to the collective interests of the 'nation' below and struggle constantly to create consensus. This ideology permeates not just the privately owned media, but has become the accepted wisdom in all the major social institutions, for example in the education system as well as in public broadcasting. The BBC developed in close relationship with the state and under Reith it came to embody in its language and programme content a form of liberal capitalist ideology. In practice this was the belief that the class system was basically sound and that as long as working people 'knew their place' they were capable of improvement by gradual exposure to 'high culture'. The benign aspect of this ideology was revealed as no more than a veneer when the working class forgot its place in the General Strike of 1926. Statements by Reith, who was Director General at the time, are very revealing about the role of broadcasting when class relations and class antagonisms become overt. A critical issue in the strike was whether the state should commandeer the BBC and run it as a propaganda agency in defence of the 'public' interest. Reith opposed this and sought formal autonomy on the grounds that the BBC could fulfil the required function more effectively as a politically independent body. In the end, the state and broadcasting reached a mutually acceptable compromise which exists to this day. Reith commented in his diaries:

The cabinet decision is really a negative one. They want to be able to say that they did not commandeer us, but they know that they can trust us not to be really impartial.*

At this time, and throughout the early years of the BBC, journalists were disciplined and socialised into a distinctive style and ethos. Professor Tom Burns writes in his history of the organisation:

Throughout the 1930s the BBC was ridden with a tight rein. Mild as the incursions by commentators into foreign politics and genteel as discussions between political figures were, there were frequent occasions on which objections were raised in the House and in the press to what were labelled errors in editorial judgement or lapses in taste. Such occasions reinforced the propensity of the chief officials of the BBC to prove themselves even more 'reliable'; and, as ever, self-censorship proved to be the most effective form of censorship.

(*The BBC: Public Institution and Private World*, Macmillan, 1977, p. 17)

One of the lapses in taste which Burns cites concerned a BBC producer who was disciplined by the Director General. He was warned never again to commit so serious an error of judgement as to allow hunger marchers to speak on the radio and say what they thought of the government. The Talks Department, which carried programmes on the condition of the unemployed in the 1930s, allowed people to speak for themselves. This brought down a torrent of criticism from the government and what had been a genuine attempt at social investigation on radio gave way to less contentious programmes.

The BBC came to embody a view of the world from the perspective of the powerful. The extent to which the

*The Reith Diaries, E.C. Stuart (Ed.), Collins, 1975, p. 96.

population at large is likely to acknowledge the correctness and legitimacy of this view will vary according to the period, the state of the economy, and above all the level of class antagonism which exists. At the start of the General Strike, for instance, the TUC warned its members against believing the BBC. And at the present time, there is some evidence that there is a steady decline in audience confidence in national television news broadcasting. In the periods of most intense social conflict there have appeared radical alternative media with substantial audiences. It is important to examine their origins and struggle for survival in the face of commercial competition.

Radicalism and Conservatism

The radical press in the 1830s formed around trade union struggles and programmes for political change. Although it was illegal and subject to intensive persecution by the state it had a much wider readership than the establishment press of the time. One paper, *The Destructive,* carried this editorial which stated the aims of the new press:

> Some simpletons talk of knowledge as rendering the working classes more obedient, more dutiful ... But such knowledge is trash; the only knowledge which is of any service to working people is that which makes them more dissatisfied and makes them worse slaves. This is the knowledge we shall give them.*

The radical press has grown and declined more or less in relation to the periods of radical agitation in our society. *The Daily Herald,* a labour paper, had in the thirties the biggest daily circulation in the world. The demise of *The Daily Herald* shows very clearly the problems of sustaining a radical press in the face of commercial competition. It was constantly drained by the fact that a mass circulation paper depends substantially on advertising. For the quality press this is on average 58% of its revenue. The radical press has not received anything like this kind of subsidy, partly for political reasons and partly because its readership has been too poor to be of much interest to advertisers. There have been many direct political

* Bronterre O'Brien writing in 1836 quoted in S. Harrison, *Poor Men's Guardians,* Lawrence and Wishart, 1974, p. 103.

intcrventions by such interests. In 1956 *The Guardian* was almost alone in opposing the British invasion of Suez and rapidly lost 40% of its advertising revenue. *The Daily Herald* suffered constantly from this lack of advertising and collapsed even though it had a readership of 4.7 million. This was twice the total for *The Guardian, The Times* and *The Financial Times* put together. It is clearly easier to sustain a radical press in periods of intense political and social agitation because working people are prepared to pay more for it and go to greater lengths to obtain it. The mass-produced establishment press is always likely to be cheaper. It is backed by large capital and even if it makes a loss can be subsidised by large corporations for their own interests. In addition, this press suffers no problems with distribution — (unlike *Private Eye* it will not be banned by W.H. Smith). For similar reasons *The Liverpool Free Press,* which was for several years Britain's biggest-selling alternative local paper, was not available in a majority of Liverpool newsagents. It is in periods of political and social calm, either after major defeats or in periods of economic boom, that the radical press has the most difficulty. At such times the existing order is likely to be regarded by most people as legitimate, or at least unavoidable.

In any case, some subordinate groups are likely to see themselves as having a vested interest in the existing order. People who work for finance capital in the traditionally more secure occupations, in banking or insurance, have not been as severely hit by the recessions which have affected industrial manufacturing. Even among productive workers there are divisions between 'skilled' and 'unskilled' which are reflected in different attitudes at work and to employers. The 'unskilled' unions when they first developed were very radical, while those of the 'skilled' workers tended to defend the privileges that they had won without seeking a major change. Other groups have also come into being whose whole existence depends on the maintenance of the status quo, for example, the forces of the army and the police and large sections of the civil service. These sections of the population are more likely to concede the legitimacy of the existing order, but nevertheless their consent cannot be taken for granted — it has to be worked for. The privately owned press and public and commercial broadcasting are crucial agencies which on a day-to-day basis attempt to

secure the consent of these groups and the acquiescence of the
working class as a whole.

Political conflict and agitation is always in a 'more or less'
state. It is the effect of the consensual ideology to make it less
rather than more. But this ideology is not something handed
down by a 'ruling class' to quiescent and gullible working
people. To make sense to the mass audience, even to its most
conservative sections, it has to connect with the things that
people have struggled for — with their real beliefs and
aspirations. The existing ideology is therefore closely
connected with the major concession of the welfare state and
the notion that economic and social management can gradually
modify the worst excesses of market capitalism. This idea, that
all social and economic problems have a solution, reached its
height under the Conservative administrations in the boom
and affluence of the 1950s. It appeared to many that living
standards for all social classes would gradually improve and
that consumerism would replace radicalism. In this period the
state had become responsible for the orchestration of this new
relation between labour and capital. There was to be no 'them
and us' anymore, and each worker might expect a house and a
car and, if all went well, eventually a cocktail cabinet that
lighted up. From this period all parties were committed to
growth and full employment — a commitment which is now
having to be abandoned as capitalism has moved once more
into recession and crisis. However, until recently, the
provisional and temporary nature of this accommodation of
interests was rarely recognised, and its normal underlying
strains and stresses were ignored: they were no longer
supposed to exist.

Consensus in Trouble

This is the background to the contradiction that public
broadcasting now finds itself in. It is committed to an
ideological perspective which is founded on the view of
consensus, 'one nation' and 'the community', while having to
report phenomena which cannot be fitted easily into this
framework of understanding. The broadcasters attempt to
relay ideas which are already more or less present and interpret
them for what they mistakenly see as a 'mass' audience. But to

secure this consensus they have to make sense of new and
difficult social and economic trends like unemployment,
investment collapse and inflation. This involves giving
meaning to events, facts and figures by providing explanations,
stating causes, and by editorial comment.

"Now to be less serious for a moment, did you know that an attempt
is being made on the world tripe eating contest, today?"

The change in government to the Conservatives in 1979 is a
good illustration of the problem the media face in maintaining
a coherent, consensual view. This was difficult enough with the
economics of Healey and the Treasury, but at least the Social
Contract had a semblance of being an 'agreement' with
something in it for everyone. But the BBC is distinctly
unhappy with the politics of the new right and the rise of
Thatcherism. However hard they try they cannot work out
how to say 'we are all pulling together' in the face of 3 million
unemployed. Their natural territory is the right wing of the
Labour Party or the Social Democrats. These offer once again
the prospect of an economy with an orderly working class,
whose leadership negotiates with government for the
appropriate concessions. The popularity of the Social
Democrats with the broadcasters comes from a heartfelt desire
for a return to such politics. The policies of the new right, by
contrast, are awakening the slumbering giant and raising

demands for political alternatives that the BBC had long ago
pretended did not seriously exist. In fact the acquiescence of
the working class in the existing system was never total*.
During the most 'consensual' periods some political groups
openly sustained a radical commitment and various shades of
radicalism remained in the unions and the Labour Party. At the
base of society attitudes to the legitimacy of the new order
were very ambivalent. Militancy over wages and the growth of
a strong shop stewards' movement had for years coexisted
uneasily with the generalised belief in the 'national interest'
and an apparent decline in political initiatives.

Now economic decline is bringing increased agitation. In the
face of this, broadcasters will still attempt to secure some form
of agreement by pressing the politics of social democracy and
by closing off access to radical explanations of what society is
and how it could work. This may be done routinely and quite
unconsciously as long as the people are not demanding social
and political alternatives on any large scale. In industrial
coverage, the Leyland case study shows how alternative
explanations were quite routinely closed off in favour of the
'normal' explanation that it was the fault of the workforce. But
if crisis and dissent intensify, then a more direct control may be
necessary.

Keeping in Line

The development and fine-tuning of consensual ideology can
be related in part to conscious policy decisions by senior
broadcasters. The state of news broadcasting in both the BBC
and ITN is constantly monitored from above. Its direction and
content are sometimes subject to quite direct interventions,
and this is shown by the minutes of senior committee meetings
at the BBC. A complete set of these was recently leaked and re-
printed in *The Leveller* magazine. In these, the top
management discuss, for example, how a new phase of

*This is in part reflected in the way in which the privately owned
press is marketed across sections of the working class. One national
newspaper, *The Daily Mirror,* although owned by a multi-national
company has for many years supported the Labour Party and has
pursued 'moderate' left policies.

economic crisis might mean new restrictions on news output:
The Editor of News and Current Affairs said that at the present
juncture stories about this country's currency needed careful
handling ... he was inclined, for the first time in his career to
suggest that they should always be checked first with the
Treasury ... It would be wrong in the present circumstances to
put out a major news story of which the Government had no
warning.

(The Leveller, January 1978, p.15)

Such direct and overt interventions are comparatively rare in
most areas of reporting. The official line is likely to emerge and
be changed through much more informal processes, such as the
routine contacts between journalists and civil servants.
Journalists are highly dependent on Whitehall as a major
source of information, especially on the economy, industry and
foreign affairs. Press briefings in this context are likely to be
manipulative and journalists who do not toe the line are
subject to the ultimate sanction of not being given
information. Control as direct as this is again only a rare
occurrence, since most top journalists share a similar social and
cultural background with the hierarchies of the state. More
importantly, the routine working practices of journalists are
informed by the class assumptions of the society in which they
live, that some people are more important than others and have
a greater right to speak. In a recent article in the *New
Statesman* we expressed this as follows:

> When television journalists want to know something important
> about the economy or industry, it seems natural to them to ask
> an 'important person': a senior civil servant would fit the bill, or
> a government minister.
>
> (*New Statesman*, 6.4.79)

Two weeks later, Richard Francis, the Director of News and
Current Affairs at the BBC replied to our article and simply re-
affirmed what we were saying. He wrote:

> ... the BBC's journalists do indeed find it natural to ask 'an
> important person' — a senior civil servant or government
> minister, for instance — for they are the people whose decisions
> largely determine how things will be run in our democracy.
>
> (*New Statesman*, 20.4.79)

The fact that most of the sources that journalists consult in
the Treasury, Whitehall, the Department of Employment, the
Foreign Office, *etc.*, are all *unelected*, but still wield a great
power in their own right, had completely passed him by. Even
if they were elected, their views on policies would still only be
political *opinions* and should not be treated by journalists in
the manner that Moses received the tablets at Mount Sinai.
This assumption about who has the right to speak and what is
an important information source means that quite contentious
information, about how the economy is working and what
might be done about it, is packaged up and presented as merely

factual. As we show in the Social Contract case study the latest statistical information on the 'causes' of inflation is presented routinely alongside the latest *political* view by a Cabinet Minister or a chairman of the Price Commission.

Economic Interests

Alongside such specific pressures on the content of the media there are clearly some which emerge from fairly crude material interests. The pressure for programmes which make money is seen at its purest in the history of American television. In the 1950s companies that were sponsoring programmes actually complained about television drama which showed people living fulfilled lives in spite of being poor. To be happy without commodities was regarded as fundamentally un-American. In addition the demand for high audience ratings at the cheapest cost has led to 'formulae' for producing long-running series with the same basic characters and plots. If one was a 'success' in the ratings then another twenty like it would follow. Single plays were taboo, since anything which 'ended' meant that viewers would change channel and perhaps not come back. Thus we have *Dallas* and *Crossroads* which go on for months or years, with each show having a dramatic 'hook' at the end, so that viewers will turn on next week.

The tedium and repetition of formula westerns, detective stories and comedy shows comes because they have in the end to be basically the same. This is so that people can pick up the plot when they switch from channel to channel as the adverts come on. Central characters frequently repeat what has happened so far, since in America there are very long advertisements about every eight minutes. The idea is to 'catch' people as they move channel. Hence on *Star Trek*: 'Captain's log, star date 10/5, we have landed,' *etc.* Such pressures affect British programming, since commercial companies here are also searching for ratings, and more significantly are making major series with the intention of exporting them to the American market. The style and content of programmes is affected when television is run simply as one part of a business conglomerate. At present 'independent' television in Britain is controlled by companies such as Granada. It has major interests in television rental, cinema exhibition, bingo, social clubs, the music industry and book publishing. Other TV holding companies have had interests in areas such as film production, insurance and property.

Although economic interests are important the institutions of the media and certainly of public broadcasting cannot be seen as merely relaying ideology from the state or private capital. The media institutions and the journalists they employ do have some autonomy. They usually wish to claim that their reportage is accurate and trustworthy, although as we show in the case studies the unconscious political assumptions which they hold produce selection and distortion which often invalidate these claims. Still, the journalists certainly do not see themselves as being passive mouthpieces, and at times actively dissociate themselves from establishment figures. This may take the form of arguments with individual politicians, for example the rows between Harold Wilson and the BBC over how much he was making on his book royalties. But such arguments are likely to be conducted on an individual level: the media may challenge politicians but not the political or economic system. In the same way it may look at 'isolated' abuses in the economy — it may investigate 'pockets of poverty' or the effects of unemployment in a single area but not usually the nature of the economy which produces these.

There may be pressures in the media to engage in a more fundamental criticism, and this is more likely at times when there is overt social conflict and civil disorder. Because journalists themselves wish to be autonomous from the state and 'private' interests, a case such as Northern Ireland creates real problems. The media authorities and the state cannot always rely on reports being within the normal limits, because working journalists are forced to make conscious decisions between two obviously contradictory positions. The views and activities of those involved in a violent attack on the state and the lived experiences of the people caught up in that struggle cannot be readily fitted into the orthodox view: that an orderly, peaceful society could exist, but for the activities of a small minority of extremists. This contradiction is intensified for British journalists because of the enormous difference between what they are supposed to report and what is passing as normal coverage in countries such as America.

The American Broadcasting Corporation, one of the three major American networks, recently put out in one of its few documentary slots a one hour programme entitled *To Die for Ireland*. This could simply not be shown in Britain — in fact the British government even protested about it being shown in America. It is important in that it shows quite clearly some alternative perspectives on Ireland. The programme begins by setting the problems of Ireland in their colonial history:

For centuries all of Ireland was ruled by Great Britain until the Irish Republican Army took up guns in 1916 to seek independence. To end the bloodshed Britain divided; into a free, largely Catholic republic to the south, and a Protestant dominated British province to the north.

As a result of the division, the Catholics in Northern Ireland became a minority denied equal status in jobs, housing and government.

(ABC *To Die for Ireland*, 1980)

Because the programme started in this way, opposition to the British state and the presence of troops can no longer be seen as an abnormality. Words like 'small minority', 'terrorists', 'thugs', 'bully-boys', 'cowardly murderers', no longer fit as readily. The Army and the IRA are interviewed as opposing military forces, and the definition of who are the terrorists is up for discussion. The editor of the Sinn Fein newspaper is interviewed and speaks as follows:

The British have used the media as an extension of their war machine in Ireland to prevent us appearing, let's say, on television or to prevent the Republican interpretation of events ... The IRA, we believe, are of course an army of liberation, and that army has a legitimate right to use what means are at its disposal. We believe those means should be explained — of why there is an IRA and what they hope to achieve. I mean, as far as we're concerned, the only terrorists in Ireland are the British Army.

They are the people here responsible for the torture, responsible for the massive repression, and the ones who have for seven hundred years, in fact, misruled this country. So, they are the real terrorists, and they are the men of violence.

Civil rights organisers, such as Father Denis Faul, are also interviewed.

We've got a verdict of the European Commission on Human

Rights recording torture, a verdict of the European Court of Human Rights recording cruel and inhuman and degrading treatment against hundreds of people. We have two reports from Amnesty International, and then you have the British ... the British reports themselves. The list is endless. The situation doesn't improve. And the British Army here have the widest scope of draconian emergency laws available to them, possibly in the world — outside of maybe the Iron Curtain countries, but maybe even including them. How can the Army or the British hope to achieve a consensus of sympathy, when they are abusing the law continually?

American reporters in this programme are able to ask British troop commanders how their men feel about patrolling an area such as Crossmaglen where the local population have, in the main square, erected a statue in support of the IRA.

In British programming, the authorities have had to engage in quite direct censorship and control in order to prevent the alternative perspective surfacing in anything more than a fragmentary and incoherent way. The combination of pressures from the base and the obvious existence of the alternative accounts in foreign coverage has put many journalists in a real dilemma. There has been a series of controversies and disciplinings on the question of Ireland.

"... AND IN NORTHERN IRELAND
TONIGHT, A SOLDIER WAS SHOT
        BY TERRORISTS, AND A
YOUNG GIRL DIED AFTER AN
INCIDENT INVOLVING A PLASTIC
BULLET... "

There are over 20 documented cases of outright external interference and internal repression by the broadcasting authorities. For these to emerge at all as a public debate meant that individuals jeopardised their careers. The case of Colin Thomas illustrates the tensions which exist in the BBC. He had worked there for 16 years and recounts how he was incensed by the criticisms that were being made of the coverage of Ireland. He resolved to 'take up the gauntlet' and show how a good programme could be made. He began work on a series entitled *The Irish Way* and eventually resigned in May 1978 over the degree of censorship and pressure to which he was subjected. In his programme's commentary on how different people in Ireland thought about the crisis, he had felt obliged to indicate that a large number saw the problem as a colonial one, and viewed the British troops as an army of occupation. The final issue on which he resigned was over a shot of a woman in Londonderry, who visited the grave of her son daily. On the grave the words "Murdered by British Paratroopers on Bloody Sunday" were inscribed. According to Thomas this was the general feeling in the village and to have left it out would have been to distort. But it was, of course, one shot amongst many which had to go. According to Thomas it went on the instructions of the Controller of BBC 1. The BBC commented on the affair: "This was essentially a process of editorial assessment and judgement on the part of the producer. In no way can it be regarded as censorship." (*The Sunday Times*, May 1978).

Both the press and broadcasting are active and quite consistent in their support of powerful, established interests, and promote a 'social democratic' consensus. Information is both controlled and routinely organised to fit within a set of assumptions about how the world works and how it ought to work. The media relay the ideology appropriate to a population which is relatively quiescent, and actually promote that quiescence by limiting access to alternatives. We might expect such an overt defence of established interests from a privately owned press, but a publicly owned broadcasting system is bound by both legal and conventional constraints to be both balanced and impartial. It ought to look more open, pluralistic and less partisan than the conservative press. In fact our research shows that it does not.

Broadcasters claim in their own defence that they are merely reflecting what most people actually believe. They are, as they

say, believers in parliamentary democracy. But even within the
limits of the consensus and what they define as legitimate
debate they clearly give preference to some opinions over
others. Furthermore, they process 'factual' information
incorrectly to justify these viewpoints.

There are still three criticisms which the broadcasters have
yet to answer. First, they do not reflect the existing range of
views in a balanced fashion. They neglect whole areas of
opinion — upgrade some and downgrade others. As we show in
the case studies, new areas of 'chosen' political and economic
opinion were actually sold to the people, and coverage was
organised to legitimise these political views. In other words,
even within the range of 'sanctioned' debate, the broadcasters
are clearly very choosy.

Second, they are undemocratic in their choice of who is
allowed to speak and who is defined as important. Unelected
officials such as senior civil servants are routinely consulted.
This is not a 'balanced' reflection of a democratic consensus.
Broadcasters are obsessed with hierarchies and allocate status
and importance in terms of their own class assumptions. Low
status individuals are filmed differently and their opinions are
often sought simply as a back-up to the dominant view.
Women will rarely be interviewed in 'serious' news
programmes unless they are being used as a form of chorus, for
instance when they oppose a strike. A high proportion of news
coverage of women is likely to be about either the Queen or
Margaret Thatcher. These assumptions on who has the
'normal' right to be consulted mean that the broadcasters have
difficulty in dealing with any form of grass-roots movement.

Finally, by seeking to process information within what they
take to be the consensual view they violate their own canons of
accuracy and impartiality. There is a range of arguments about
how the economy and society work, which cannot be resolved
merely by an appeal to what most people think. Their
resolution clearly depends on empirical evidence: for example,
on whether wages really are ahead of prices, and if they are,
does this mean they are causing inflation? The selection and
editing of information to fit a dominant view cannot be
justified by saying that this view is held by a lot of 'important'
people.

The essential thrust of our critique is not against media

workers as such, as if we could have better news simply by getting better journalists, editors and producers. Rather, it relates to the picture of society that the media construct with such remarkable consistency. We attribute this artificial and one-dimensional picture to the nature of organisations whose basic assumption is that our industrial, economic and social system operates to the benefit of everyone involved. Such a vision is given in the name of 'public interest', but unfortunately its construction involves the mass of this 'public' being misrepresented.

VII
WHAT NEXT?

The ability to organise mass communication in our society is the exclusive preserve of a small number of people. Whether this is because the media are privately owned or because they are indirectly controlled by the state, the fact is that the majority of the population are unable to participate or exercise any form of democratic control. Communications in our society *appear* to be free. Anyone with capital can set up a newspaper: the public then has the choice to buy it or not. The broadcasting institutions are a 'public' service and formally separated from direct state intervention. But there are two immediate reasons why this has not ensured 'free' communication in our society. The first is that in practice the media as a whole process information around a limited world view. There is no sense in which all views of how our society works, or prescriptions for changing it, enjoy equal access or are given equal credibility. The second is that the media are remote and unresponsive. The debate about free communication must confront the issues of access, accountability and control. These have always been central issues surrounding both press and broadcasting. We look here at a range of positions that have been taken on what's wrong with broadcasting and what might be done about it.

Leave it to the Professionals?

When broadcasters are criticised about programme content some take refuge behind the claim of professional expertise. Appealing to skill, knowledge and tradition they argue that

improvements can be made merely by tightening up existing
practices. Some deny that any fundamental change in either the
organisation or practice of broadcasting is required. This is
especially evident in the case of the news. Selection and
presentation are seen as self-evident and self-justifying
outcomes of professional wisdom and 'news sense'. A recent
BBC pamphlet argues:

    The news value of a story is something immediately
    recognisable, intuitively sensed by a journalist who has been

schooled in provincial or national newsrooms ... The 'graduates' of that school soon learn to spot the significant news point, the relevant detail, the interesting human touch, which distinguish the newsworthy story — the material with news value or news merits — from the candidate for the sub-editor's spike.

> (*The Task of Broadcasting News* — a study for the BBC General Advisory Council, published by the BBC, May 1976, p. 12)

This denies the possibility that news is a product of contentious values and judgements — that what is 'significant', 'relevant', 'merely interesting', is always the product of definite social and political ways of understanding the world.

Broadcasters also tend to invoke the argument about professionalism in answer to the charge that they are unresponsive and remote. It is claimed that their professional knowledge and sensitivity will ensure that the full range of social and political debate in our society will be represented. The broadcasters are best fitted to decide who will get on and what they are able to say.

The evidence above, however, demonstrates a systematic flow of television news that routinely excludes wide sections of the population from television news. Such bad news does not result from a *lack* of professionalism. It is a product of the routine application of professional norms. Indeed, broadcasters have claimed the exclusion of large sections of the population from television news as a professional virtue — it is 'natural' in their view to concentrate on the views of the powerful. Access for such groups, especially government or 'official' sources, is one part of the way news production is organised. Favoured journalists are given special briefings via the 'lobby system' — only certain journalists are allowed to attend. The dismantling of such organisational restrictions on free information is in itself an important reform.

Government Scrutiny

At present the accountability of British broadcasting is provided by the IBA and the BBC Board of Governors. Established by Act of Parliament, these bodies consist of

government appointees. Their role is supposed to be the
regulation of broadcasting in the 'public interest'. The state
has the power to instruct the BBC Board of Governors and the
IBA to broadcast or withdraw whatever it wants. This has not
been necessary in practice because the interests of the state and
the broadcasting institutions are not fundamentally antagonis-
tic. The members of the BBC Board of Governors and the IBA
are drawn from a narrow and unrepresentative section of the
population. They are selected from a list drawn up by the
Director of the Public Appointments of the Civil Service. It
contains around 4,000 names of people deemed by successive
governments to be sufficiently trustworthy to sit on
government commissions. The practice of these bodies over
the reporting of Northern Ireland provides striking evidence
of the class backgrounds of their members and their
relationship to the interests of the state. When issues arise in
broadcasting that are deemed sensitive, the IBA and BBC
Board of Governors know exactly where they stand. They
follow the tradition established by Reith in the reporting of
the General Strike.

The Campaign for Free Speech on Ireland have documented
numerous occasions where bans, cuts and delays to
programmes have been imposed. One such programme was
Thames' *In Friendship and Forgiveness*. The programme was
made on the occasion of the Queen's Jubilee visit to Northern
Ireland on 10 and 11 August, 1977. It was intended to counter
the pervasive media picture of a trouble spot now at peace for
this visit. The programme was banned two minutes before
transmission on August 12. After some small alterations, it was
finally transmitted on 26 and 27 August at a variety of times in
the ITV regions. Such a relationship with the interests of the
state means that the broadcasting authorities are secretive and
unaccountable. For example, the IBA awards franchises to
private broadcasting companies in secrecy, except for token
public meetings. The nature of these indicates what the IBA
considers to be due participation and accountability. Though
they are often well attended, these meetings have obscure and
arbitrary rules and procedures. As Jonathan Coe reported in
the *New Statesman* on 26 September, 1980, the criteria by
which the IBA select organisations to put their point of view
are somewhat mystifying. In Bristol a representative from one

of the city's largest Asian youth organisations asked why his organisation had *not* been approached. In Ayr a woman from the Kilmarnock Flower Circle wanted to know why her organisation *had* been approached.

The BBC and IBA have both attempted to give the appearance of accountability and responsiveness by setting up advisory councils. These consist of people chosen by the BBC and IBA who meet four times a year. The members have no secretaries or research facilities and the proceedings are held in secret. The public does not know what advice has been given or whether it has been taken. The problem, then, with the institutionalised mechanisms to ensure public accountability is that they further shroud the private world of broadcasting from public scrutiny. They offer only a fiction of independence and accountability.

Government Commissions

The media are also subject to periodic scrutiny by government enquiry. There have been three sets of these since the Second World War. The most recent was the Annan Commission on the Future of Broadcasting established in 1974. It was to examine the existing performance of broadcasting and debate its future structure.

Under some pressure from Labour members it did include criticisms of television news, and argued:

That the coverage of industrial affairs is in some respects inadequate and unsatisfactory is not in doubt. Difficult as the reporting of industrial stories may be, the broadcasters have not fully thought it through. They too often forget that to represent management at their desks, apparently the calm and collected representatives of order, and to represent shop stewards and picket lines stopping production, apparently the agents of disruption, gives a false picture of what strikes are about.

This is not much more than a criticism of sloppy journalism. It questions only the extent of professionalism, rather than the nature of professional practices themselves. Thus the report continues:

The broadcasters have fallen into the professional error of putting compelling camera-work before the news. Furthermore, the causes why people come out on strike are often

extraordinarily complex. No reporter does his job adequately if
he interviews only the leading shop steward or union official.
The fact that a strike is not backed by the union does not
exonerate broadcasters from discovering why the work force is
out. The Glasgow Media Group reported that in the unofficial
Glasgow dustcart drivers' dispute in 1975, during 13 weeks and
21 interviews shown on the national news none of those on
strike was interviewed.

> (Report of the Committee on the Future of Broadcasting
> HMSO, p. 272)

For us this was not a lapse of professionalism or a careless
omission, but a denial of access that was a logical outcome of
the manner in which television news processes information.
When the Commission confronted this central issue, it
decided there was no charge to answer on the grounds that
broadcasters found such a suggestion "bewildering" and
resented it.

On the issue of public accountability and diversity Annan
was more adventurous. The Commission proposed the
establishment of two new bodies; a Broadcasting Complaints
Commission which would supplement the internal machinery
of the IBA and BBC to adjudicate on complaints and be
empowered to award costs if they were upheld. The second
proposed body was to be a Public Enquiry Board for
Broadcasting, holding public hearings on specific issues and
regular audits on the performance of broadcast authorities and
the future awarding of franchises. In addition the Commission
proposed that a fourth TV channel be operated by an Open
Broadcasting Authority. It would provide diversity by
transmitting programmes made by independent producers as
well as educational and other material from individual
companies. Such a proposal may have provided for a degree of
access and a wider range of programmes from those outside the
monolithic institutions of the BBC and IBA. These limited
proposals for the fourth channel, however, were rejected by the
Conservative Government elected in 1979. They were
committed to allowing further inroads into broadcasting by
private capital. Unless there are strong pressures against it, the
fourth channel is now likely to imitate ITV I.

The Question of Democratic Control

The debate on public broadcasting has revolved around suggestions that either there should be more state control or broadcasting should be diversified by selling it off to private interests. An awkward choice is thus generated between more state bureaucracy, or a private ownership of the media geared to 'market needs' and profitability. Private ownership of broadcasting places the right to determine public tastes and needs in the hands of powerful economic interests. The grafting on of additional supervisory bodies or replacing the existing ones merely opens up broadcasting to the individuals who sit on these committees. It simply substitutes one form of state control for another and does not ensure *popular* accountability. Given that broadcasting is too important to be left in the hands of broadcasters how can it be opened up to democratic participation?

The tight central control of the BBC and the IBA, along with the power of private capital in the British broadcasting industry, is unique in Europe for its non-recognition of the political and cultural pluralism of modern society. A necessary reform is that the strong state control of the BBC and the IBA should be dismantled. This must occur alongside the removal of 'independent' broadcasting from commercial domination, and the democratisation of the controlling bodies. There is a need for new structures which are representative of the plurality of British society in terms of class, sex, ethnic and other groups. Such institutions should be responsive and open to democratic control at a community, regional and national level.

The Aims of Broadcasting

Social and political opinions in our society do not enjoy equal access and status in the media. The problem, however, is not only one of correcting inaccuracies, as the Changing Television Group* have written:

> For many the solution to these complaints is simple. Since the media are seen as presenting a distorted picture of the real world, then all that is required is a change of control to substitute a 'real' picture of the 'real world'. This point of view avoids the

central problem. However fair and even handed the programmers or the programming, the problem remains that all media will inevitably be biased, whoever controls and operates them, because media represent the world through a process of selection, rejection and creation. The problem then is not 'how to represent the real world in a real way', but rather 'how to represent and recognise the different, often conflicting, views of the 'real world' which exist within society and within the mass media themselves'. Equally important, how can these different views and interpretations be brought into the open rather than masked by a mythical cloak of impartiality?

In practice, the problem of balance is resolved by a broadcasting establishment favouring and enforcing a version of British society in which the norm is harmony and in which conflict is an aberration. A new definition of the aims of broadcasting should be established which recognises the conflicts of interests between groups and lays a duty on broadcasters to represent these differences fairly and accurately. Broadcasters should have a duty to produce programmes from the different perspectives within society. At the same time there should be positive moves within broadcasting to combat racism and sexism. We do not believe that broadcasting 'freedom' should extend to those groups who would harm others on the basis of their sex or colour of skin.

But this alone will not act as an adequate safeguard against misrepresentation. Assumptions about news and other programmes should not be defined only by professional journalists and broadcasters. Hence moves to redefine the aims of broadcasting must be accompanied by its democratisation.

Control

The IBA and BBC are too centralised, too closely linked with

* The suggestions for change set out here have been worked out with the Changing Television Group (an *ad hoc* group of television producers and researchers) whose aim is to work towards more democratic media. We have drawn on its document *Changing Television*, which can be had from the group at 14 Rosaville Road, London SW6.

the state and remote from the general population. It is unacceptable that the controllers of the broadcasting system should be drawn from such a narrow layer of our society. As a first step parliament should appoint governing bodies that are broadly representative of the class, ethnic and sex composition of our society. But as a long term aim democratisation of broadcasting should occur at local and regional levels. Boards should be *elected;* these would provide delegates to a national conference which would act as the supreme authority in broadcasting. The local, regional and national boards should hold their deliberations in public, supervise the granting of franchises, editorial appointments, and the financing of broadcasting.

It is essential that the ability of private capital to control large sections of our broadcasting network should be stopped. Broadcasting in our society has been regarded by some as a licence to print money and commercial priorities have come before providing a genuine community service. Television has become one part of the interests of large conglomerates who control anything from steak houses to hotel chains. The local and regional boards should award franchises to non-profit making groups. The boards would then be empowered to supervise the performance of television staff and investigate complaints. These boards would have no rights to pre-broadcast censorship on individual programmes. In addition they should pursue with the franchise holders the broad aim of maximising access to broadcasting.

Access

Our evidence shows a systematic denial of access to the media both at the level of who can appear, and who is allowed to make programmes. At present access is restricted to token off-peak programmes with tiny budgets compared to 'main stream' broadcasting. Minority groups that are at present disregarded should be allotted programme space with full editorial control. Access programmes would be particularly appropriate to areas of conflict in our society. Such programmes can give people a real chance to make their case and may replace the crude stereotypes which at present pass for grass-roots opinion.

Complaints and Feedback

The local, regional and national broadcasting boards should hold regular public meetings to examine existing programming and discuss absences in the output. These bodies would also consider appeals for a right to reply. For example, our evidence has shown that television news systematically frames industrial disputes in such a way that those groups pursuing industrial action are seen as irresponsible and disruptive. Where distortion occurs groups should in principle have the right of redress.

Broadcast material is a public resource, it should be a legal requirement that a copy of all broadcast material be lodged in a national archive open to all members of the public. In addition, the public should have access, on request, to complete transcripts of broadcasting material in order to formulate complaints.

Making Programmes

No one would seriously maintain that in a literate society people should be denied pens and paper. Yet this restriction effectively operates on broadcast technology in our society. Its most potent form of communication technology is in the hands of a tiny number of people. A proportion of broadcast material could be supplied by non-professional sources. National, regional and local machinery should be set up to encourage and finance such material. Courses on operating communications technology should be available inside schools, colleges and community centres.

Inside Television

It is unacceptable that professional broadcasters be drawn from a narrow section of our society. We must change a situation in which a company such as Thames Television — which services Brixton, Southall, Lewisham and Deptford — has only a small percentage of its workforce who are black people, many of whom work in catering. A policy of positive discrimination should be adopted for women and ethnic minorities. It is essential to recruit people who can speak from a *range* of political and social perspectives.

The present organisation of news around narrow economic and political viewpoints produces a journalism which is inaccurate and unprofessional. A part of improving this would be to familiarise journalists with a wider range of perspectives on our society. There should be an emphasis on in-service training in areas such as economics, politics, sociology and trade union studies to increase the level of expertise.

Free Information

The freedom of journalists to investigate the powerful is directly controlled by the state. The Official Secrets Act makes it possible for governments to define a wide range of information as being beyond the scrutiny of journalists and the public. The government also has a 'voluntary' system of restricting access to information through the 'D–Notices' Committee. This is composed of government representatives, permanent civil servants and senior members of the media who reach 'agreements' on the suppression of information deemed to be sensitive. D-Notices are supposed to relate to defence but in practice operate as another general restriction on working journalists. Such constraints would limit for example reports on the extent of US involvement in running European nuclear weapons systems and who has the responsibility for starting a war. In addition, such control leaves the activities of whole branches of the Civil Service totally above question. Direct interventions using these controls are comparatively rare because journalists tend to produce material that stays on the right side of them. Self-censorship tends to become the norm. This structure within which journalists work must be changed. One improvement would be a Freedom of Information Act which would guarantee access to all areas of information vital to the public interest, and that is in our view a necessary prerequisite for a free journalism.

Minimum Demands

Aims of Broadcasting: Broadcasters should be required to represent fairly and accurately the divisions within our social world resulting from class, race or sex, and programmes should be made from the perspectives which result from these divisions.

Control: To put the new aims into practice, the present Board of Control should be made more representative of the class, racial and sexual composition of our society. Ultimately, Boards should be elected at local and regional levels.

Access: A major part of the output should be given to forms of access programming, with proper budgets allocated to these. Material from non-professional sources should also be featured, and broadcasting authorities should encourage the development of resources in the community to produce this.

The background and affiliations of the professionals who at present make programmes, should be broadly representative of the outside society. There must be positive discrimination in the recruitment of women and ethnic minorities to rectify existing imbalances.

Here and Now — What to do, where to join, how to complain

The distortions and inaccuracies which come from the present organisation of broadcasting should be challenged as they occur. It is important to argue with journalists about their products. Some are sympathetic and will welcome complaints and comments from outside. Some are not, and need telling very forcefully that at present the portrayal in the media of working people and political ideas is a travesty. Of course, broadcasting will not alter simply by changing the minds of individual journalists, but nonetheless it is important to work with those who will listen. The pressure from the outside lends support to those who are working for better television within the organisations. There are already some important developments inside. The television technicians' union (ACTT) is pressing hard for change and has re-established its committee to monitor bias in television. Recently we have seen how the tacit threat of strikes by the NUJ changed the attitude of the BBC management to the Carrickmore incident and persuaded them to show the *Panorama* programmes on the security services. In addition, The Campaign for Press Freedom* has brought together a large number of different groups and unions in the demands for the setting up of a Labour Press and the 'Right of Reply' to material published in the privately owned papers. The CPF is now turning its attention to broadcasting as well, and the extension of the Right of Reply to television and radio will be an important first step.

It is crucial that local organisations and trade unions keep up steady contact with journalists. Where specific issues arise, such as a strike, then press handouts and prepared 'copy' should always be provided. This can go on alongside the development of 'alternative' local media and news sheets. It is

* Information and membership can be had from Campaign for Press Freedom, 274/288 London Road, Hadleigh, Essex SS7 2DE. Other organisations working for change in specific areas are: Women's Broadcasting and Film Lobby, 46 Warwick Avenue, London W9; Women in Media, 21 Stratford Grove, London SW15; Campaign against Racism in the Media, P.O. Box 50, London N1.

probably not worth bothering with the very right-wing press, but those journalists who will try to use material properly should be kept informed. A very good book giving advice on this and on how to contact the press, television and radio is Denis MacShane's *Using the Media* (Pluto Press 1979). Sometimes, meetings with journalists can be organised by local unions or trades councils. The Glasgow Media Group was involved in organising such a meeting between BBC current affairs producers and a group of trade unionists from Glasgow and Manchester. The people from the unions spent about three weeks looking at television programmes about the 1980 steel strike and made a series of detailed criticisms of the coverage. They then argued about these for a whole day in the BBC at Lime Grove. This is something that could be done frequently through all of the different local television services. The Changing Television Group is at present working to organise such activity. The key to organising such criticism is to arrive at a clear idea inside the group as to what exactly is incorrect or partial in news coverage. This has to be distinguished from what people simply find unacceptable or unpleasant on television. The views of particular politicians, for example, may be thought distasteful, but television cannot be blamed simply for reporting them. It only becomes possible to complain when some views are taken up, endorsed and used as the *organising principle* for coverage.

Grounds for Complaint

There are two principal grounds of complaint: 'accuracy' and 'balance'. The first of these is always the most powerful. We have often found that in giving its preferred view, television 'squeezes' information to fit. Trade unionists frequently know more about their own industry or dispute than journalists and can comment on factual errors.

At the time of the TUC's 'day of action' in May 1980, a number of television reports carried stories of all the industries that were still working and had thus ignored the TUC call. For example one report commented that 'four of the nineteen Scottish pits worked on' (*Reporting Scotland* 14.5.80). Someone who worked in this industry might find this a strange way to express action in which the great majority of pits were on strike. This was on the local section of *Nationwide*. After a number of complaints that evening, the main report on *Nationwide* twenty minutes later appeared as: "Only four out of nineteen Scottish mines were operational." (*Nationwide*, Scottish reporter, 14.5.80).

What gave these complaints their force was that the earlier report had been run alongside a quite inaccurate attack on nationalised industries. It was by an economics correspondent who had commented:

> Such industrial disruption as there has been, has been concentrated in the nationalised industries — the coal mines, the docks and the railways. But far from being bad for the economy, it is possible to argue that the temporary closure of these concerns could be a bonus.
>
> *Nationalised industries run up losses every day of the year* of twelve million pounds, most of which is in their wage bill, so this week they will be saving a huge sum, leaving Mrs. Thatcher's finances that bit better off.
>
> (Reporting Scotland 14.5.81)

It was pointed out immediately afterwards on the telephone to the BBC that this was a false vision. The National Coal Board had not in fact lost money in the previous year, and a number of other nationalised industries such as gas, oil, tele-communications and electricity all make substantial profits. This 'economics' was not much more than a political broadcast.

In twenty minutes, the tenor of the report from Scotland changed from the earlier account, which focused largely on the *lack* of support for the day of action, to one which discussed the severity of the closures 'in important areas'. In this short period, even the number of people on the Glasgow demonstration dramatically increased. On *Reporting Scotland* we heard that: "Police estimated that between eight and ten thousand people turned up." But on *Nationwide* the Scottish region reported: "This afternoon in Glasgow, up to fifteen thousand demonstrators turned up to display their anger at government policies."

In formulating complaints, arguments about 'balance' are more difficult to establish, since each individual programme is not required to give an absolutely equal account. In other words the television companies argue that 'balance' can be spread across a number of programmes — for example, the news might do a major profile each night of the different candidates in an election. This usually means it is necessary to look at a number of programmes before reaching conclusions, but sometimes it is possible to see severe imbalances in a relatively small area of coverage. 'Preferred' viewpoints are given a higher status and are more likely to feature in headlines, summaries or interview questions. Views that are included for 'token' balance are more likely to be somewhere in the middle. For example a strike story might run as follows:

HEAD: The Print dispute: Lord Creed speaks out.

NEWSCASTER: Lord Creed has said tonight that the unions cannot view his organisation as a bottomless well from which to draw money. A report from our industrial correspondent ...

INDUSTRIAL CORRESPONDENT: This is a stern message ... disruption ... Print losing money ... exports lost ... I asked a shop steward when he might expect a return to work.

SHOP STEWARD: It's hardly our fault that we are not in work, since this is actually a lock-out. It is really just another example of a multi-national hiving off its profitable assets and closing down those that it doesn't want.

INDUSTRIAL CORRESPONDENT: ... Still deadlocked tonight ... no sign of agreement ... *etc.* This is News at Three, Print Street.

NEWSCASTER: And now the nun who sang puppies to sleep ...

Some hours later as transmission closes the news headlines for the day are read:

And in the Print dispute, Lord Creed said tonight that the unions could not view his organisation as a bottomless well from which to draw money.

And in Washington, President ...*etc.*

Those who have the time to make such comparisons might well ask, what happened to the shop steward? Why are his comments not in the headlines alongside those of the owner. What stops the late summary appearing as:

Lord Creed said tonight that the unions could not view his organisation as a bottomless well from which to draw money, but the Father of the union chapel says that this is just another example of a multi-national hiving off its profitable assets and closing down those it does not want.

A further example is the coverage of an actual factory

closure in the north of England. It was pointed out by
Margaret Thatcher at the time as an example of workers
pricing themselves out of jobs, since it had shut in the middle
of a wages dispute. Both ITN and *Nationwide* began with her
views. When the shop stewards were interviewed on
Nationwide it was apparent that they believed the
management to be using the dispute as an excuse to shut the
factory and save money. They said that: "This place was gonna
close and they've done it on the cheap, they've done it without
paying any redundancy."

We asked some of the journalists involved why they could
not begin such reports with a simple headline giving both
views. For example:

Mrs. Thatcher says, 'Workers are pricing themselves out of a
job', but the workers say, 'It's a fix'.

They said it was simply not possible within the conditions of
their own work, even though the journalists that we spoke to
actually believed the workers' argument. One described his
own organisation in this case as "trotting along like poodles
after Mrs. Thatcher". This is why a barrage of complaints is
necessary to support those journalists who do have the
alternative information, but who are not allowed to use it
properly. The existing rules of who is important enough to
initiate stories or appear in headlines must be challenged from
the outside.

The key issue in terms of balance is clearly not that trade
unionists are absent from the screen. In some senses, they and
their actions are quite over-exposed. The main complaints are
the context in which their views appear, the way in which their
actions are explained by journalists and the use of them by
television to make political points. Often, shots of strikes or
pickets are no more than wallpaper for a superimposed
commentary. In the steel strike of 1980, the alleged problem of
'flying pickets' was a favourite subject. A BBC *News Special*
brought together a great deal of news film on this. In it, the
pickets are quite freely accused of "intimidation", without any
chance to reply:

JOURNALIST: (over shots of pickets) There's no doubt that
that kind of intimidation and the massive police involvement it
entails strengthened the government's determination to bring in
their Employment Act.

and later:

> So an undoubted win for the pickets. Hadfields was indeed closed down for a time amid charges of wholesale intimidation and ever increasing demands for a change in the law to prevent it.
>
> (BBC *News Special Steel Strike* 1.9.80)

"... CAMERA TWO, CLOSE UP ON THE BLOOD, CUT TO FLYING PICKETS, CAMERA FOUR, DISGUSTED STRIKERS' WIVES. CUT TO INTERVIEW WITH CHIEF CONSTABLE, ROLL THE COMMENTARY, "HOW MUCH MORE CAN PUBLIC STAND?"..."

Although the film begins and ends with shots of pickets, and they are very much central characters, there is no point at which any of them actually appear on the screen and say why they are picketing or what has led to the trouble with the police.

Such imbalances should be the subject of immediate complaints. The procedure for television news is simply to write or phone and ask for the duty officer. Explain the complaint and ask for it to be confirmed to you in writing. The addresses and phone numbers are:

BBC Television,   ITN,
Television Centre,   48 Wells Street,
Wood Lane, London W12   London W1
01-743 8000   01-637 2424

If you have the energy it is also worth phoning and asking for the newsdesk, where it is possible to talk directly to people who have worked on the programme.

One of the provisions of the recent Broadcasting Act was a new body, the Broadcasting Complaints Commission, independent of either the BBC or the IBA. The address and phone number is:

Broadcasting Complaints Commission,
20 Albert Embankment,
London SE1
01-211 8473

The Commission has powers to demand evidence from the broadcasters and in theory at least can accept for adjudication a wide range of complaints from organisations as well as individuals. It is the only place of appeal outside the broadcasting organisations against gross mis-presentation and breach of the impartiality requirement. Transcripts of individual programmes can be obtained by asking local MPs to order them through the House of Commons Library.

"Hundreds of hysterical journalists, eager for knocking copy, today descended on picketing strikers at . . ."

A Recent Complaint

On 2 April 1981 the Glasgow Group wrote to the BBC and the IBA pointing formally to the existence of bias in television.

The letter cited the recently published *More Bad News* as
evidence of the serious imbalance in the coverage of industrial
and economic affairs. It was also signed by over 100 university
professors, trade union leaders and MPs. These included
Raymond Williams and Joan Robinson of Cambridge
University; Stuart Hall of the Open University; and E.P.
Thompson, the historian. It was also endorsed by Professor
Stuart Hood, who was for a time the deputy head of BBC
News, and by 73 MPs, including Tony Benn, Michael Meacher,
Bob Crier, Ian Mikardo and Joan Maynard. The General
Secretaries of 22 major unions signed, including both of the
major broadcasting unions as well as Moss Evans (TGWU),
John Boyd (AUEW), Alan Fisher (NUPE), David Basnett
(GMWU), Geoffrey Drain (NALGO), and Joe Gormley of
the NUM.

The central demand of the letter was that the evidence of
bias be shown in television programmes. This request
occasioned an intense debate inside the organisations. The
confidential minutes of the BBC's News and Current Affairs
meeting were sent to the Glasgow Group. They document the
extensive argument which took place about the letter and the
work of the Glasgow Group. They reveal a keen desire to be
seen to be taking criticisms seriously. The Director of News
and Current Affairs is referred to as saying:

> He had no qualms about the impartiality of the BBC's news
> bulletins; *it was however important that the BBC should be seen to
> be taking criticisms of shortcomings seriously.* With this in mind,
> DNCA invited the comments of the meeting in two areas: the
> first was on the general question of how the BBC should reply to
> the charges of the Glasgow group; the second related to the
> *confidentiality of the proceedings of the meeting.*
>
> (BBC News and Current Affairs Minutes 7.4.81)

The real problem that the BBC apparently faces is that people
are beginning to believe criticisms of them — even their own
trainees were suspect. One senior producer is reported as
agreeing that:

> ... there had never been an occasion in the past ten to fifteen
> years when the trade union movement and the Labour Party had
> trusted the broadcasters. However, he did not think it enough
> to say as (others) had done earlier that the public generally had
> confidence in the BBC's reporting. He strongly supported the

suggestion that the BBC should commission some research into its coverage, and that the BBC *should be seen* to consider it important to do so. The allegations made by the Glasgow group and others were permeating deeply into the consciousness of the general public, even down to influencing the way some of the BBC's own news trainees based their appreciation of its news coverage.

                                        (NCA Minutes 7.4.81)

Our own view is that evidence of bias and critical comment should of right be shown on television. The demand for this could be taken up by local union and labour branches, and by other groups who suffer sexual or racial disadvantage. For over six years our research unit and others have compiled evidence pointing to severe breaches in the requirements of impartiality and balance. It is not acceptable that this work should be the subject of so much private attention by broadcasters, while they remain silent on a medium which is supposed to be publicly accountable.

Television will not alter unless it is pressured to do so. There are many who work within it who are unhappy with its organisation and content. But they will remain isolated unless the demand for change is voiced loudly by the unions, inside and outside television, and through the political instruments of labour. Broadcasting is too important to be ignored, and it is foolish to wait for changes in other parts of society before demanding that it live up to requirements of accuracy and balance. It will not change until the population, who are misrepresented and who suffer the effects of bad news, demand instead truly democratic media.

SOME USEFUL BOOKS

General

J. Curran, M. Gurevitch & J. Woollacott (Eds), *Mass
Communications and Society* (Edward Arnold)
J. Curran & J. Seaton, *Power without Responsibility – the Press
and Broadcasting in Britain* (Fontana)
J. Downing, *The Media Machine* (Pluto Press)
S. Hood, *On Television* (Pluto Press)
D. MacShane, *How to Use the Media* (Pluto Press)
Minority Press Group, *Here is the other News* – challenges to
the local commercial press.
Where is the Other News? – the news trade and the radical
press.
The Other Secret Service – press distribution and press
censorship.
Rolling Our Own – women in printing, publishing and
distribution.
Brian Whittiker, *News Limited* – why you can't read all about
it.
(The above five titles are available from: Minority Press
Group, 9 Poland Street, London W1)
P. Schlesinger, *Putting 'Reality' Together* (Constable)
D. Morley & C. Brunsdon,*Everyday Television: 'Nationwide'*
(British Film Institute Publications)

Media and Racism

Campaign Against Racism in the Media, *In Black and White*
(CARM, P.O. Box 50, London N1)

S. Hall, C. Critcher, T. Jefferson, J. Clarke & B. Roberts,
Policing the Crisis (Macmillan)
P. Hartman & C. Husband, *Racism and the Mass Media*
(Davis Poynter)
C. Husband (Ed), *White Media and Black Britain* (Arrow)

Media and Ireland

Campaign for Free Speech on Ireland *The British Media and
Ireland - Truth: The First Casualty* (1 Northend Road,
London W14)
P. Schlesinger, chapter in *Putting 'Reality' Together*
(Constable)

Media and Law and Order

S. Chibnall, *Law and Order News* (Tavistock)
S. Hall *et.al.*, *Policing the Crisis* (Macmillan)

Media and Women

Centre for Contemporary Cultural Studies, *Women Take
Issue* (Hutchinson)
M. Stott & J. King, *Is this your life?* (Virago)